tax planning *and* compliance *for*
tax-exempt organizations
sixth edition

T0338310

Update Service

BECOME A SUBSCRIBER!

Did you purchase this product from a bookstore?

If you did, it's important for you to become a subscriber. John Wiley & Sons, Inc. may publish, on a periodic basis, supplements and new editions to reflect the latest changes in the subject matter that you *need to know* in order to stay competitive in this ever-changing industry. By contacting the Wiley office nearest you, you'll receive any current update at no additional charge. In addition, you'll receive future updates and revised or related volumes on a 30-day examination review.

If you purchased this product directly from John Wiley & Sons, Inc., we have already recorded your subscription for this update service.

To become a subscriber, please call 1-877-762-2974 or send your name, company name (if applicable), address, and the title of the product to:

mailing address: **Supplement Department**
John Wiley & Sons, Inc.
10475 Crosspoint Blvd.
Indianapolis, IN 46256

e-mail: **subscriber@wiley.com**
fax: **1-800-605-2665**
online: **www.wiley.com**

For customers outside the United States, please contact the Wiley office nearest you:

Professional & Reference Division
John Wiley & Sons Canada, Ltd.
90 Eglinton Ave. E. Suite 300
Toronto, Ontario M4P 2Y3
Canada
Phone: 416-236-4433
Phone: 1-800-567-4797
Fax: 416-236-8743
Email: canada@wlley.com

John Wiley & Sons Australia, Ltd.
42 McDougall Street
Milton, Queensland 4064
AUSTRALIA
Phone: 61-7-3859-9755
Fax: 61-7-3859-9715
Email: aus-custservice@wiley.com

John Wiley & Sons, Ltd.
European Distribution Centre
New Era Estate
Oldlands Way
Bognor Regis, West Sussex
PO22 9NQ, UK
Phone: (0)1243 779777
Fax: (0)1243 843 123
Email: customer@wlley.co.uk

John Wiley & Sons (Asia) Pte., Ltd.
1 Fusionopolis Walk
#07-01 Solaris South Tower
SINGAPORE 138628
Phone: 65-6302-9838
Fax: 65-6265-1782
Customer Service: 65-6302-9800
Email: asiacart@wiley.com

tax planning *and* compliance *for*
tax-exempt organizations
sixth edition

Rules, Checklists, Procedures

2024 CUMULATIVE SUPPLEMENT

Jody Blazek

WILEY

Copyright © 2024 by John Wiley & Sons, Inc. All rights reserved.

Published by John Wiley & Sons, Inc., Hoboken, New Jersey.
Published simultaneously in Canada.

No part of this publication may be reproduced, stored in a retrieval system, or transmitted in any form or by any means, electronic, mechanical, photocopying, recording, scanning, or otherwise, except as permitted under Section 107 or 108 of the 1976 United States Copyright Act, without either the prior written permission of the Publisher, or authorization through payment of the appropriate per-copy fee to the Copyright Clearance Center, Inc., 222 Rosewood Drive, Danvers, MA 01923, (978) 750-8400, fax (978) 750-4470, or on the web at www.copyright.com. Requests to the Publisher for permission should be addressed to the Permissions Department, John Wiley & Sons, Inc., 111 River Street, Hoboken, NJ 07030, (201) 748-6011, fax (201) 748-6008, or online at http://www.wiley.com/go/permission.

Trademarks: Wiley and the Wiley logo are trademarks or registered trademarks of John Wiley & Sons, Inc. and/or its affiliates in the United States and other countries and may not be used without written permission. All other trademarks are the property of their respective owners. John Wiley & Sons, Inc. is not associated with any product or vendor mentioned in this book.

Limit of Liability/Disclaimer of Warranty: While the publisher and author have used their best efforts in preparing this book, they make no representations or warranties with respect to the accuracy or completeness of the contents of this book and specifically disclaim any implied warranties of merchantability or fitness for a particular purpose. No warranty may be created or extended by sales representatives or written sales materials. The advice and strategies contained herein may not be suitable for your situation. You should consult with a professional where appropriate. Further, readers should be aware that websites listed in this work may have changed or disappeared between when this work was written and when it is read. Neither the publisher nor authors shall be liable for any loss of profit or any other commercial damages, including but not limited to special, incidental, consequential, or other damages.

For general information on our other products and services or for technical support, please contact our Customer Care Department within the United States at (800) 762-2974, outside the United States at (317) 572-3993 or fax (317) 572-4002.

Wiley also publishes its books in a variety of electronic formats. Some content that appears in print may not be available in electronic formats. For more information about Wiley products, visit our web site at www.wiley.com.

Library of Congress Cataloging-in-Publication Data:

Names: Blazek, Jody, author.
Title: Tax planning and compliance for tax-exempt organizations : rules, checklists, procedures 2024 cumulative supplement / Jody Blazek.
Description: Sixth edition. | Hoboken : Wiley, 2024. | Includes index.
Identifiers: LCCN 2023057876 (print) | LCCN 2023057877 (ebook) | ISBN 9781394253654 (paperback) | ISBN 9781394253678 (adobe pdf) | ISBN 9781394253661 (epub)
Classification: LCC KF6449 .B58 2024 (print) | LCC KF6449 (ebook)
LC record available at https://lccn.loc.gov/2023057876
LC ebook record available at https://lccn.loc.gov/2023057877

Cover Design: Wiley
Cover Image: © Lugiaz/Shutterstock

SKY10068015_022324

To all the wonderful nonprofit clients, seminar participants, and fellow CPAs and lawyers who serve nonprofits and ask me the questions that inspire my study and research and provide fuel for my books.

Contents

List of Exhibits

Preface

This 2023 Cumulative Supplement starts with significant announcements that impacted tax compliance work for lawyers and accountants (who work with private foundations).

- On June 1, 2023, the IRS began accepting e-filed determination letter applications on Pay.gov. The IRS continued to accept paper Forms 5307 and 5316 through June 30, 2023. Now those forms will also have to be e-filed.
- In a News Release, the IRS has warned businesses to be wary of aggressive Employee Retention Credit (ERC) marketing. The IRS urges businesses to watch out for red flags that can signal trouble.[1]
- The IRS has released an Employee Retention Credit eligibility checklist to help businesses and tax-exempt organizations determine if they qualify to claim the ERC.
- Readers may gain caution in reading the three reviews of the court consideration regarding Short Stop Electric[2] focused on deduction of interest expense vs. its capitalization, accrued expenses for cash-basis taxpayer, and allocation of personal vs. business use of assets.
- Abbreviations designating types of Treasury Department pronouncements and rulings now include GLAM, in addition to PLR, TAM, and RP. A GLAM is a generic legal advice memo issued by the Office of Chief Counsel, not binding as tax code but usable as precedence regarding tax matters. Compared to a PLR, or private letter ruling that is an IRS response to a specific taxpayer question that, although it cannot be relied on, it is binding on the IRS.

---

[1] IR 2023-170, 9/14/2023.
[2] Short Stop Electric, Inc., v. Commissioner, (2023) TC Memo 2023-114.

About the Author

Jody Blazek was a founder and partner in Blazek & Vetterling (BV), a Houston-based CPA firm focusing on tax, auditing, and financial planning for exempt organizations and the individuals who create, fund, and work with them. BV serves more than 600 nonprofit organizations providing audits and other financial reports, tax returns and compliance, and planning services.

Jody began her professional career at KPMG, then Peat, Marwick, Mitchell & Co. Her concentration on exempt organizations began in 1969, when she was assigned to study the Tax Reform Act that completely revamped the taxation of charities and created private foundations. From 1972 to 1981, she gained nonprofit management experience as treasurer of the Menil Interests, where she worked with John and Dominique de Menil to plan for and manage the Menil Collection, the Rothko Chapel, and other projects of Menil Foundation. She reentered public practice in 1981 and started the firm she now serves.

She is the author of six books in the Wiley Nonprofit Series: *Tax Planning and Compliance for Tax-Exempt Organizations 6th edition* (2020). *Nonprofit Organization Financial Planning Made Easy (2008), Revised Form 990* (2012), and *IRS Form 1023 Preparation Guide* (2005). She also coauthored with Bruce R. Hopkins, *Private Foundations: Tax Law 5th edition* (2020) and *The Legal Answer Book for Private Foundations* (2002).

Jody was a past chair of the Tax-Exempt Organizations Resource Panel and a member of Form 1023 and 999 Revision Task Forces for the American Institute of Certified Public Accountants. She serves on the national editorial board of *The Exempt Organization Tax Review* and is a member of the Volunteer Service Committee of the Houston Chapter of Certified Public Accountants. She is a founding director of Texas Accountants and Lawyers for the Arts and a member of the board of the Anchorage Foundation of Texas and Houston Artists Fund. She is a frequent speaker at nonprofit symposia, including AICPA Not-For-Profit Industry Conference and Private Foundation Summit; Heckerling Institute on Estate Planning; University of Texas Law School Nonprofit Organizations Institute; Texas, New York, and Washington State CPA Societies' Nonprofit Conferences; and Institute for Board Development among others.

Jody received a BBA from the University of Texas at Austin in 1964 and took selected taxation courses at South Texas School of Law. She loves to swim, go to the beach, and grow organic vegetables. She and her husband, David Crossley, nurture two sons, Austin and Jay Blazek Crossley, and their wives and three grandchildren.

Acknowledgments

The response to the fifth edition of this book was positive and encouraging; I am grateful for the opportunity to comprehensively update and to consider many issues in more depth. In 1969, when KPMG gave me the task of studying, interpreting, and communicating the new private foundation rules to our Houston clients, I began a search for information to interpret the nonprofit organization tax laws and procedures and often found it lacking. This book represents a compendium of checklists, client memoranda, and interpretive materials developed over the years to provide guideposts for compliance and tax planning for exempt organizations.

My experience has been enriched by a myriad of wonderful people with ideas for improving the human condition and saving the earth. The wealth of altruism and kindness shared by benefactors and volunteers in the nonprofit community is an inspiration. From the vantage point of the funder who wants to create a private foundation, the healer who senses the ability to cure a disease, and the artist who wants to paint a public mural, among many others, I have had the privilege of working with many people to figure out the best financial and tax mode in which to establish an entity that can accomplish those goals. My years as a KPMG tax specialist under the able tutelage of John Herzfeld and Lloyd Jard taught me that tax rules are not black and white; answers are complex and often gray. Achieving the best tax answer requires an exacting search, an ability to weigh alternatives, and the willingness to defend your choice.

As treasurer and chief financial officer of the Menil Foundation and The Rothko Chapel—the Houston-based charitable ventures of Dominique and John de Menil—I had a unique hands-on opportunity to manage nonprofit organizations. Returning to public practice in 1981, I continued my commitment to nonprofit organizations and started an accounting firm that focuses on exempt organizations and the people who work with and create them. In the early 1980s, a group of professionals created the Texas Accountants and Lawyers for the Arts (TALA). Our purpose was to improve the technical expertise and expand the body of law applicable to nonprofit organizations. With this goal in mind, seminars were organized and technical issues researched and reported. Since that time, the number of trained and willing volunteers with TALA and other pro bono organizations has multiplied many times. This book is partly a result of the questions asked as I teach continuing education seminars. It is intended to be a practical guide to establishing and maintaining taxexempt status for nonprofit organizations.

I also acknowledge the people who played an instrumental role in making this book possible. Bruce Hopkins, my coauthor for private foundation books, and Wiley editor Jeffrey Brown, in 1988, found merit in materials I proposed for the first edition of this book. Over the years, I have benefited from accomplished Wiley editors such as Marla Bobowich and Martha Cooley. Susan McDermott, my current editor and Brooke Graves pushed me to prepare this sixth edition and provided encouragement and invaluable assistance. Jennifer MacDonald, development editor, performed miracles in reviewing our manuscripts, and Melissa Lopez, production editor, combed through the maze of checklists, exhibits, and appendixes, greatly facilitating the process. Thanks to all of you.

On a professional level, I am indebted to my colleagues at Blazek & Vetterling who with me serve our more than 600 nonprofit clients. The countless questions our clients and other professionals present to us provide the fuel for materials considered and I thank them as well. Since 2001, I have had the enriching experience of serving as an advisor to Foundation Source. Working with their senior vice president for Legal Affairs, Jeffrey Haskell, I have been confronted with a wonderful array of private foundation questions. Assisting them to develop policies and procedures for an online administrative system for foundations has been a challenging and invaluable learning experience.

Finally, I am indebted to my husband, my sons, and my clients for their patience and support while I devoted time to this project.

Distinguishing Characteristics of Tax-Exempt Organizations

p.4. Add after third paragraph:

The Christ Ambassadors Church was not recognized at tax-exempt (c)(3) organization by the IRS or the Tax Court. The available descriptions of its activities and modest amount of money involved make one wonder whether there is more to this case than reported. The activities reported on Form 990 included:

- "Assisting individuals with therapy, food pantry, group therapy assistance, individual with therapy, food pantry, group therapy, and after school tutoring to help the less privileged." (Part II, line 1)
- "Assistance to the public by providing food and medical assistance to the less fortunate and mentally retarded patients in Las Vegas Nevada." (Schedule O)
- The organization claims public charity status as a church. Schedule A, Part I, box 1. Petitioner operated the 501(c)(3) exempt organization as a church to assist the community with spiritual and other needs.

Christ Ambassadors Church operated a behavioral health clinic. Donations and monies from the behavioral health clinic were used to, among other things, operate the church, bring congregants to and from church events, and purchase food and necessities for the homeless and hungry of the greater Las Vegas, Nevada area.

The IRS's revocation letter said, "Our adverse determination as to your exempt status was made for the following reasons: You have not established that you are both organized and operated exclusively for charitable, educational, or other exempt purposes within the meaning of IRC § 501(c)(3). Additionally, your primary activity is the provision of behavioral health services to those that can pay. You are operated in a commercial manner with substantial income-producing activities of a kind normally conducted by nonexempt commercial entities. You have not established that you continue to qualify for tax-exempt status as a church or that your church activities were not secondary and incidental to your overall operations. Furthermore, part of your earnings inured to the benefit of your officers and their family members, which constitutes inurement prohibited under IRC § 501(c)(3). For all these reasons, you fail to meet the requirements for tax exemption."

p. 4. Sources to identify qualifying Exempt Organization

The amazing list of organizations that qualify as tax-exempt organizations according to the IRS should be carefully reviewed on Exhibit 1.1 Organization Reference Chart. Note the chart takes four pages in the original book. Additionally lists can be found in the following publications on the Internet.

- **Publication 78.** An online version of IRS Publication 78 can be found on the IRS website. Referred to as Pub 78 by most, it allows taxpayers to search check to see if a charitable organization qualifies for tax-IRS Publication 78 (Cumulative List of Organizations) lists organizations that have been recognized by the IRS as eligible to receive tax-deductible contributions. The list is not all-inclusive and does not show every qualifying organization. This is now searchable on the IRS website on Tax Exempt Organization (https://apps.irs.gov/apps/oes/). Organizations may be searched by name or tax ID number.
- **GuideStar Charity Check Data Sources.** GuideStar acquires all IRS data directly from the IRS.
- **IRS Internal Revenue Bulletin** (IRB) lists changes in charitable status since the last Publication 78 release. Between the release of IRS Publication 78 and the subsequent IRS Internal Revenue Bulletin, the IRB date will reflect the most recent release date of IRS Publication 78.
- **IRS Business Master File** lists approximately 1.7 million nonprofits registered with the IRS as tax-exempt organizations.
- **IRS Automatic Revocation of Exemption List** contains organizations that have had their federal tax-exempt status automatically revoked for failing to file an annual return or notice with the IRS for three consecutive years.
- **Foundation Status Code** is a value derived by mapping the codes found on the 990PF filing instructions to the corresponding codes in the IRS BMF. Note that not all codes are able to be mapped due to insufficient data.
- **Office of Foreign Assets Control (OFAC) Specially Designated Nationals (SDN)** lists organizations that are owned or controlled by targeted individuals, groups, and entities, such as terrorists or narcotics traffickers. Their assets are blocked and U.S. persons are generally prohibited from dealing with them.

CHAPTER 1.3

p. 13. Add as opening text:

A June 26, 2023, article entitled "The 2022 Giving Slump Exposes the Fragility of Top-Heavy Charity," is causing many involved in philanthropic programs to wonder. According to the author, "wealthy donors have taken more and more control over our charitable sector, while increasingly distressed households of everyday Americans drop off the donor rolls. This results in problems for working charities: one is donor control over mission and two is money being funneled away from active charities into intermediaries such as foundations and Donor Advised Funds.[1]

A coalition of leaders from the fields of higher education, health care, philanthropy, law, and nonprofit governance have called upon the IRS to require large nonprofits to make public the composition of their governing boards. In an Open Letter, the Coalition for Nonprofit Board Diversity Disclosure specifically requests that the IRS include on tax form 990 a question about "the gender and racial/ethnic demographics of their boards, based on how board members self-identify." It further supports "including LGBTQ+ and disability disclosure." More than 140 organizations and individuals interested in the governance and operation of nonprofit organizations and committed to the value of diversity throughout organizations have joined the growing Coalition to date.

The Open Letter emphasizes that gender and racial gaps persist in nonprofit board rooms, including those of some of the country's largest universities and hospitals. It also reveals the difficulty that even researchers have obtaining data about nonprofit boards. The IRS, the letter asserts, is best positioned to collect and make public this data as the agency that already asks questions about nonprofit boards and governance practices. The letter clarifies that requiring institutions to be transparent would not require them to change their boards; however, asking the question conveys a message that the IRS stands behind diversity as a good governance practice. Citing more than 15 years of "mainstream and highly visible organizations and publications, and countless studies and reports" on for-profit boards that show that diversity is a commonly accepted standard of good governance, the Coalition points to Nasdaq's model, approved by the Securities and Exchange Commission, that requires its listed companies to report aggregate board composition data.

Board diversity in the nonprofit sector has not generated the same degree of interest and advocacy, although a 2020 national study reports that board diversity brings benefits for nonprofits similar to for-profit organizations. "After years of scrutiny or pressure, leaders in the for-profit community have finally recognized that board diversity makes for better decisions and reduces risk," said Jane Scaccetti, CPA[2] and member of several for-profit and large nonprofit boards and signatory to the letter. "It is time for the boards of nonprofits that serve and employ diverse populations to do likewise." In the Open Letter, the Coalition makes it clear that they are asking for the one new question to be added only for those organizations that file the full Form 990, not the Form 990-EZ used by the smallest nonprofits.

"Board demographic disclosure will bring visibility and accountability to institutions benefiting from the designation of public charities," said Cid Wilson, president and CEO of the Hispanic Association on Corporate Responsibility (HACR) as well as chair of the Alliance for Board Diversity. "The IRS is the one entity that could require them to disclose the demographic make-up of their boards. Form 990 is an existing straightforward way to capture accurate data that will be made publicly available every year." To read and sign the letter or learn more, go to coalition-4-nonprofit-diversity.[3]

p. 15. Add report of new tax code provisions: (add to end of paragraph 1.4) without a new title.

---

[1]Helen Flannery. a researcher with the Institute for Policy studies Reform Initiative, in USA Today.
[2]Of Council, Armanino LLP. Jane is a CPA with experience in family business consulting, family wealth issues and board governance.
[3]Coalition Asks IRS to Require Disclosure of Nonprofit Board Composition.

The Inflation Reduction Act (IRA) added, modified, and extended a number of business credits for investments in clean energy technologies—and also added a "direct pay" provision, effectively making several credits reportable with their annual tax filings available to tax-exempt and many government entities as refundable credits. The benefits of these tax incentives, how they work and who is eligible for payments using examples of opportunities to use them in the exempt organization sector follows and examines some of the thornier implementation issues Treasury work through in issuing guidance.[4]

Code Sections 30C, 45, 45Q, 45U, 45V, 45V, 45W, 45Y, 45Z, 48, 48C, and 48E are all direct pay credits for which tax exempt organizations are eligible. The IRS has provided additional guidance in the form of proposed regulations, and announcements on new energy credits.

p. 14. Add IRS Priority Guidance Plan

■ **TE/GE's Priorities for FY 2024**

"Our (IRS Exempt Organization Division) FY24 program and priorities align with the IRS Strategic Operating Plan FY2023-2031 and its five transformation objectives:

■ **Service (Better Taxpayer Experience)**
■ **Issue Resolution (Faster Issue Resolution)**
■ **Enforcement (Smarter Enforcement)**
■ **Modernization (Advanced Technology and Analytics), and**
■ **Workforce (Empowered Employees)**

Better Taxpayer Experience

Dramatically improve services to help taxpayers meet their obligations and receive the tax incentives for which they are eligible.

■ Focus on proactively connecting with internal and external stakeholders to identify and better serve small and underserved taxpayers such as small entities and limited English proficiency communities to foster voluntary compliance.
■ Continue to promote the use of digital communication vehicles like Taxpayer Digital Communications (TDC) and Data Upload Tool (DUT), for secure, electronic communication with taxpayers and representatives.
■ Provide education and outreach to help TE/GE stakeholders make complete and accurate elective payment elections for clean energy credits under the Inflation Reduction Act.
■ Continue to partner with Stakeholder Partnerships, Education & Communication (SPEC) on its Native American initiative focusing on increasing access to tax services throughout Indian Country.

---

[4]EO Tax Journal—eotaxjournal@gmail.com, *May 5, 2023, remarks of Amber MacKenzie, Attorney-Advisor, Office of Tax Policy, Department of Treasury.*

Faster Issue Resolution

Quickly resolve taxpayer issues when they arise.

- Support effective processing and compliance at pre-filing and filing for elective payment elections of clean energy credits.
- Support IRS efforts to proactively review and address Employee Retention Credit claims, during the filing process or immediately after return processing.
- Collaborate across the IRS to streamline notices and improve how notices are updated and issued to taxpayers. Encourage two-way electronic communication between IRS and taxpayers regarding notices.
- Continue effort to update the EPCRS revenue procedure (Revenue Procedure 2021-30) to incorporate changes made by Sections 301 and 305 of SECURE 2.0 Act. Section 305 of SECURE 2.0 requires new guidance for the EPCRS and a new IRA correction program be published by December 2024.
- Based on the results of the Employee Plans (EP) pre-exam compliance program pilot, EP will develop a second pilot during FY 24 for the pre-exam compliance program that allows plan sponsors to self-correct qualification failures before an exam begins.
- Continue efforts to improve filing and reporting compliance within the exempt sector.

Smarter Enforcement

Focus expanded enforcement on taxpayers with complex tax filings and high-dollar noncompliance to address the tax gap.

- Collaborate with Research, Applied Analytics, and Statistics (RAAS) to continue building and refining Exempt Organizations exam case selection using advanced modeling techniques.

Advanced Technology and Analytics

Deliver cutting-edge technology, data, and analytics to operate more effectively.

- Complete and launch Form 13909, Tax-Exempt Organization Complaint (Referral) in the Digital and Mobile Adaptive Forms (DMAF) framework to allow the public to submit a referral using the electronic form accessible from any device. This will expand paperless submission options for taxpayers and provide for more accurate electronic data.
- Continue to work with RAAS to develop an artificial intelligence capability to review and prioritize referrals received on Exempt Organizations.
- Continue to support Enterprise Case Management efforts to standardize Servicewide examination processes

Empowered Employees

Attract, retain, and empower a highly skilled, diverse workforce and develop a culture that is better equipped to deliver results for taxpayers.

- Continue to focus on improving consistency in the service Human & Capital Resources provides to customers by developing a feedback mechanism for new hires to provide input on ways to improve the onboarding experience for future hires.
- Execute TE/GE's recruitment strategy by continuing to partner with HCO STARS, Workforce Planning, SB/SE, LB&I, and other BODs to host direct hiring and recruiting events across all regions.
- Create detailed/extensive career training paths for employees to use as a tool for them to reference as career milestones occur.
- Commit resources to develop and deliver quality, cost-effective mission critical core training that is focused on both individual and organizational productivity and advancement.
- Create training workshops and mentoring seminars that will focus on developing the skills that TE/GE Frontline managers need to make independent data-driven decisions.
- Continue to build a collaborative team culture by hiring and retaining a diverse, talented, data-savvy, and technology-driven workforce.
- Build community relationships by expanding outreach efforts and engaging with external stakeholders to market TE/GE and IRS careers and increase our visibility.

CHAPTER 1.4 Role of the Internal Revenue Service

p. 14. Insert new second paragraph:

The IRS statistics for 2022, the latest available, didn't reflect a level of activity one would expect given the total number of exempt organizations included on the lists of the Exempt Organizations Division. The numbers reported for the following categories included:

- Denial letters to exemption applicants sent by EO Determinations (Cincinnati)
- Rulings in response to Form 8940 Requests for Miscellaneous Determinations sent by EO Determinations (Cincinnati),
- Revocation letters sent by EO Examinations (Dallas), and
- EO private letter rulings issued by the Office of Chief Counsel, of which there were very few.

For EO denial letters issued in 2022 (latest date available), there were approximately 46 denials to (c)(3)s, 11 to (c)(4)s, 6 to (c)5s, 11 to (c)(6)s, and 27 to (c)(7)s.

Such unapproved applications were likely prepared by persons unfamiliar with the EO tax code provisions that this 900+ page book focuses on, and applicants that were clearly unqualified due to expected to provide benefits to their creators was a common theme in the denials. The total number of denials, 107, is about ½ percent of the total filed in 2022. The Form 1023-EZ submitted by many applicants comprises a large portion of the list and requires very little detailed information to request recognition as a tax-exempt. The form requests in some detail programs for grants to individuals, set asides for multi-year programs or projects, and unusual grants to nonexempt entities are often approved. Surprisingly the total number of approvals was about 80. Since Form 8940 submits information about the approximately 80 Form 8940 rulings requests submitted were approved. A comparison of the total number of applications submitted to those denied and lack of analysis of reasons for failure presumably due to IRS staff levels, could be thought of positively. Thanks for the instructions to the form, which are well written, the nonprofit community receives a goodly number of approved entities to accept donations to support their work.

There were approximately 99 revocations of exempt status resulting from EO Examinations. Many of the (c)(3) revocations were for failure to keep records or for being inactive. Most of the (c)(7) revocations were for failures to satisfy the membership requirements.

(b) New Donor Instructions. On August 27, 2023, the IRS issued a revised instruction [Announcement 2023-09] of impact on donors to a charity that loses its tax-exempt qualification. The release also contained a list of "Deletions from Cumulative List of Organizations, Contributions to Which are Deductible Under Section 170 of the Code." The announcement explained the IRS policy regarding deductibility of donations to organizations whose qualification as a § 170 organization has been revoked. The notice included the names of those revoked entities and its effective date, as illustrated below.

The IRS will not, generally, disallow deductions for contributions made to a listed organization on or before the date of announcement in the Internal Revenue Bulletin that an organization no longer qualifies. However, the IRS is not precluded from disallowing a deduction for any contributions made after an organization ceases to qualify under § 170(c)(2) if the organization has not timely filed a suit for declaratory judgment under § 7428 and if the contributor (1) had knowledge of the revocation of the ruling or determination letter, (2) was aware that such revocation was imminent, or (3) was in part responsible for or was aware of the activities or omissions of the organization that brought about this revocation.

If on the other hand, a suit for declaratory judgment has been timely filed, contributions from individuals and organizations described in § 170(c)(2) that are otherwise allowable will continue to be deductible. Protection under IRS § 7428(c) would begin on August 28, 2023, and would end on the date the court first set for in § 7428(c)(1). For individual contributors, the maximum deduction protected is $1,000, with a husband and wife treated as one contributor. This benefit is not extended to any individual, in whole or in part, for the acts or omissions of the organization that were the basis for revocation.

Name of Organization	Effective Date of Revocation	Location
Teachers Organizing Property Inc	12/29/2017	Greenville, MS
Next Level Foundation	1/1/2019	Las Vegas, NV
LWL Foundation	12/1/20218	Danville, CA
Maxcess Foundation Inc	1/1/2018	Boca Raton, FL
Matthew Kull Foundation for Healing	1/1/2018	New Milford, CT
A 2nd Cup	1/1/2019	Houston, TX
Atchafalya Bit & Bridle Club Inc	1/1/2020	Houston, TX
FCPA Community Outreach	1/1/2020	Shelton, CT
FL-AL Toy Breeds Inc	1/1/2020	Theodore, AL
Goff Moll Post Building Association	9/1/2019	Brentwood, MO
Hawaii Coral Reef and Garden	10/7/2019	Sparks, NV

CHAPTER 1.5 Suitability as an Exempt Organization

p. 15. Add at end of introductory paragraph:

Start the suitability considerations by inserting at beginning an overarching question: **Who will benefit?** The answers to the four questions are significant in determining the new organization is really necessary to accomplish the mission and whether it is qualified to be recognized for tax exemption. Are creators motivated by selfish goals? And ask if the entity is being created to accomplish a charitable purpose rather than to achieve benefits for its funders themselves and their families and friends in addition to the tax savings for their donations. An extensive consideration of this issue should be can be reviewed with discussion included in Chapter 14 entitled Self-Dealing.

CHAPTER 3

Religious Organizations

p. 60. Add at end of introduction to the chapter:

Why is tax law for churches different? Are there unconstitutional conditions for religious organizations? One counselor[1] says, "In common with other charities, religious organizations enjoy significant benefits under federal tax law, including exemptions from income tax and the ability of donors to deduct their contributions for income, gift, and estate tax purposes."[2] A subset of religious organizations consisting of "churches," which include houses of worship for all sects, and certain church-related entities also enjoy unique and significant procedural advantages. These include not having to apply to the Internal Revenue Service (IRS) for recognition of tax exemption, not having to file annual information returns with the IRS, and being subject to IRS inquiries and examinations only if the IRS satisfies certain procedural requirements.[3]

But these benefits are not costless. Also in common with other charities, religious organizations are prohibited from providing private inurement and private benefit, engaging in a significant amount of lobbying, intervening in political campaigns, promoting illegality, or acting contrary to fundamental public policy.[4] Private

---

[1]Lloyd Hitoshi Mayer. 98 *Notre Dame Law Review Reflection* S1 (2023).

[2]*See, e.g.,* I.R.C. §§ 170(c)(2) (2018) (income tax deduction), 501(a), (c) (income tax exemption), 2055(a)(2) (estate tax deduction), 2106(a)(2)(A)(ii) (nonresident, noncitizen estate tax deduction), 2522(a)(2), (b)(2) (gift tax deduction). Also see *Elvig*, 375 F.3d at 963, 968.

[3]For detailed discussions of the federal tax law definition of "church" and certain church-related entities, see generally Wendy Gerzog Shaller, *Churches and Their Enviable Tax Status*, 51 U. Pitt. Law Rev.345. 350–55 (1990); Charles M. Whelan, *"Church" in the Internal Revenue Code: The Definitional Problems*, 45 Fordham L. Rev.885 (1977).

[4]*Id.* §§170(c)(2)(C), (D), 501(c)(3), 2055(a)(2), 2106(a)(2)(ii), 2522(a)(2), (b)(2) (all prohibiting private inurement, significant lobbying, and political campaign intervention); Treas. Reg. § 1.501(c)(3)-1(d)(1)(ii) (1990) (prohibiting private benefit); Rev. Rul. 75-384, 1975-2 C.B. 204 (prohibiting promoting illegality); Rev. Rul. 80-278, 1980-2 C.B. 175 (prohibiting activities contrary to clearly defined and established public policy).

inurement refers to distributing assets or earnings for the benefit of private individuals or entities who exercise substantial influence over the organization, including if the organization pays more than fair market value for services or goods or allows rent-free use of the organization's property; private benefit refers to more than incidentally serving the private interests of any individual or noncharitable entity.[5] Lobbying means attempting to influence legislation, and political campaign intervention means supporting or opposing the election of a candidate to public office.[6] The illegality and fundamental public policy limitations, both drawn from charitable trust law deemed incorporated by Congress into the applicable federal tax statutes, apply if an organization engages in substantial activities that violate federal, state, or local statutes (usually criminal ones), or substantial activities contrary to fundamental (federal) public policy that therefore demonstrate a substantial noncharitable purpose.[7] The IRS takes the position that these limitations apply with equal force to all tax-exempt charities, including religious organizations.[8] Some religious organizations have challenged the application of the lobbying, political campaign intervention, illegality, and fundamental public policy limitations on religious liberty grounds, invoking the Free Exercise of Religion Clause of the First Amendment and, more recently, the Federal Religious Freedom Restoration Act (RFRA).[9] To date, however, federal courts have rejected these challenges, concluding that they are permissible conditions on the tax benefits enjoyed by religious organizations.

This essay reconsiders this conclusion and the arguments in support of it. One such argument is that Congress intended these tax benefits to support a charitable "program," and therefore, under general unconstitutional conditions principles articulated by the Supreme Court, Congress is permitted to refuse to provide those benefits to any organization that engages in activities inconsistent with being charitable.[10] The problems with this argument include that the tax benefits only partially and indirectly fund the activities of charitable organizations, it is questionable whether some of the limitations—particularly the lobbying and political campaign intervention limitations—are inconsistent with being charitable, and it assumes, perhaps incorrectly as Michael A. Helfand argues in his contribution to this Symposium, that general unconstitutional conditions principles should apply in the free exercise of

---

[5]See Treas. Reg. §1.501(c)(3)-1(c)(2), (d)(1)(ii) (1990); IRS. *Overview of Inurement/Private Benefit Issues in* §§170(c)(2)(C), (D), 501(c)(3), 2055(a)(2), 2106(a)(2)(ii), 2522(a)(2), (b)(2) (all prohibiting private inurement, significant lobbying, and political campaign intervention); Treas. Reg. § 1.501(c)(3)-1(d)(1)(ii) (1990) (prohibiting private benefit); Rev. Rul. 75-384, 1975-2 C.B. 204 (prohibiting promoting illegality); Rev. Rul. 80-278, 1980-2 C.B. 175 (prohibiting activities contrary to clearly defined and established public policy). See *Exempt Organizations Continuing Education Technical Instruction Program for fiscal year 1990.*
[6]See Treas. Reg. § 1.501(c)(3)-1(c)(3)(ii), (iii) (1990); *Lobbying Issues in Exempt Organizations Technical Instruction Program for FY 1996,* Judith *Kindell and John Francis Reilly and Election Year Issues in Exempt Organizations Technical Instruction Program for FY 2002,* Judith *Kindell and John Francis Reilly.*
[7]See Jean Wright & Jay H. Rotz, *Illegality and Public Policy Considerations, in Exempt Organizations Technical Instruction Program for FY 1994 and* IRS, *Activities That Are Illegal or Contrary to Public Policy, in Exempt Program Organizations Technical Instruction Program for FY 1985.*
[8]*IRS Tax Guide for Churches & Religious Organizations.* 2015.
[9]See *infra* notes 25, 31, 43, and 44 and accompanying text.
[10]Agency for International Development All. for Soc'y Int'l, Inc., 570 U.S. 205 (2013).

religion context.[11] Therefore set aside this argument to consider a different argument drawn from the relevant case law.

This alternate argument is that tax law is somehow different from other legal contexts for purposes of applying the unconstitutional conditions doctrine to religious organizations. The consistent refusal of the courts to allow free exercise of religion–based exemptions from generally applicable federal tax laws suggests this may be the case. This difference could be viewed as a strand of the increasingly disfavored view sometimes referred to as "tax exceptionalism." But upon further consideration, I argue that this difference instead fits within the more traditional compelling governmental interest and least restrictive means analysis codified in RFRA and that arguably applied in the Free Exercise of Religion Clause context before the Supreme Court's decision in *Employment Division v. Smith*.

More specifically, tax law is different because of its complex rules applicable to all individuals and entities relating to expenditures for lobbying, political campaign intervention, and illegal activity. The complexity of these rules, and the risk that granting exemptions from them for any reason would undermine their uniform and consistent application, support the conclusion that the government has a compelling interest in not allowing exemptions, and that the existing limitations imposed on tax-exempt charities, including religious organizations, are the least restrictive means to do so. As a result, constitutional and RFRA free exercise of religion rights do not require exemptions for religious organizations from these existing limitations even when such organizations are motivated by their religious beliefs to engage in the limited activities. Furthermore, while this argument does not apply to the contrary to a fundamental public policy limitation, the Supreme Court has correctly concluded that in the instances where there is a fundamental public policy, ensuring that tax-supported charities do not undermine that policy is also a compelling governmental interest and prohibiting them from doing so is the least restrictive means of furthering that interest.

3.2(a) Special Aspects of a Church

p. 69. Add at end of definition:

A Ninth Circuit opinion reversed a district court's grant of summary judgment in favor of a church. Church member Huntsman contributed substantial amounts of cash and corporate shares to the Church as tithes.[12] He claimed he relied on false and misleading statements by the Church that tithing money was not used to finance commercial projects, when in fact the Church used tithing money to finance a shopping mall development and to bail out a troubled for-profit life insurance company owned by the Church. The Church argued that Huntsman's fraud claims were barred by the First Amendment. Did the ecclesiastical abstention doctrine apply since fraud

---

[11]*See* Michael A. Helfand, *There Are No Unconstitutional Conditions on Free Exercise*, 98 *Notre Dame L. Review Reflection* (Special Issue) S50, S51 (2023).

[12]As reported in EO Tax Journal 2023-132.

claims were secular and did not implicate religious beliefs about tithing itself? Was there a need to examine Huntsman's religious beliefs about the appropriate use of church money to solve a genuine dispute of material fact as to whether the Church fraudulently misrepresented the source of money used to finance the shopping mall development?

Based on the evidence in the record, including statements by church officials and in church publications, the Church knowingly misrepresented that no tithing funds were being or would be used to finance the shopping mall development and that Huntsman reasonably relied on the Church's misrepresentations. The evidence, however, did not provide a sufficient basis for a fraud claim with respect to bail-out payments to the life insurance company. Summary judgment in favor of the Church was therefore appropriate on all claims.[13]

We (the court) generally refer to the doctrine upon which the Church relied as the "ecclesiastical abstention doctrine." *Puri v. Khalsa*, 844 F.3d 1152, 1162–64 (9th Cir. 2017). The doctrine prohibits courts from deciding "internal church disputes involving matters of faith, doctrine, church governance, and polity." *Bryce v. Episcopal Church in the Diocese of Colo.*, 289 F.3d 648, 655 (10th Cir. 2002); *Jones v. Wolf*, 443 U.S. 595, 602 (1979); and *Serbian E. Orthodox Diocese for U.S. & Can. v. Milivojevich*, 426 U.S. 696, 713 (1976). The doctrine is "a qualified limitation, requiring only that courts decide disputes involving religious organizations 'without resolving underlying controversies over religious doctrine'."

In support of its First Amendment argument, the Church contended that "Huntsman objects to the use of any Church funds for City Creek." The Church selectively quotes from Huntsman's brief and misrepresents the nature of his claim. Huntsman does not object to the use of Church funds for the City Creek Mall project. Rather, he objects to how the Church represented the project would be funded. Huntsman contends that the Church solicited tithes from him by misrepresenting the purposes for which the tithes were being and would be used. Specifically, Huntsman contends that the Church denied that tithing funds would be and were used to pay for the City Creek Mall project when, in fact, tithing funds were being used for that purpose.

The ecclesiastical abstention doctrine protects First Amendment rights by avoiding court entanglement "in essentially religious controversies" or the state intervening on behalf of a particular religious doctrine. *See Serbian E. Orthodox Diocese*, 426 U.S. at 709. But these "considerations are not applicable to purely secular disputes between third parties and a particular defendant, albeit a religious affiliated organization, in which fraud . . . [is] alleged." *Gen. Council on Fin. & Admin. of the United Methodist Church v. Superior Ct. of Cal., Cnty. of San Diego*, 439 U.S. 1355, 1373 (1978) (Rehnquist, J., in chambers). That is because "under the cloak of religion, persons may [not], with impunity, commit frauds upon the public." A court or jury can assess Huntsman's reliance by looking to the Church's and Huntsman's evidence to ask if Huntsman reasonably relied on the Church's statements.[14]

---

[13]*James Huntsman v. Corporation of the President of the Church of Jesus Christ of Latter-Day Saints.*
[14]*James Huntsman v. Corporation of the President of the Church of Jesus Christ of Latter-Day Saints.*

CHAPTER 4

Charitable Organizations

4.6 Promotion of Health

p. 92. Add at end of introduction:

In recent years states have begun develop new laws that allow hospitals to reduce programs and increase fees that provide community benefit. Clearly their concern is to control costs, but that results in reductions in healthcare services for the needy. Some hospitals operate like business conglomerates. For example, a hospital in Pennsylvania faced a lawsuit to restore services to the needy. The ruling sent a warning shot to all nonprofit hospitals, highlighting that their state and local tax exemptions, which are often greater than their federal income tax exemptions, can be challenged by state and local courts. The public school system in Pottstown, Pennsylvania, had to scramble in 2018 when the local hospital, newly purchased, was converted to a tax-exempt nonprofit entity. The takeover by Tower Health meant the 219-bed Pottstown Hospital no longer had to pay federal and state taxes on any profits it made. Additionally the community hospital no longer had to pay local property taxes, taking away more than $900,000 a year from the already under-funded Pottstown School District. The school district, about an hour's drive from Philadelphia, had no choice but to trim expenses. It cut teacher aide positions and eliminated middle school foreign language classes. "We have less curriculum, less coaches, less transportation," said Superintendent Stephen Rodriguez.

The school system appealed Pottstown Hospital's new nonprofit status, and earlier this year a state court struck down the facility's property tax break. It cited the "eye-popping" compensation for multiple Tower Health executives as contrary to how Pennsylvania law defines a charity. The court decision, which Tower Health is appealing, stunned the nonprofit hospital industry, which includes roughly 3,000 nongovernment tax-exempt hospitals nationwide.[1] "The ruling sent a warning

---

[1]Andy Miller and Markian Hawryluk, *KFF Health News,* July 11, 2023.

shot to all nonprofit hospitals, highlighting that their state and local tax exemptions, which are often greater than their federal income tax exemptions, can be challenged by state and local courts," said Ge Bai, a health policy expert at Johns Hopkins University.

The Pottstown case reflects the growing scrutiny of how much the nation's nonprofit hospitals spend—and on what—to justify billions in state and federal tax breaks. In exchange for these savings, hospitals are supposed to provide community benefits, like care for those who can't afford it and free health screenings. More than a dozen states have considered or passed legislation to better define charity care, to increase transparency about the benefits hospitals provide, or, in some cases, to set minimum financial thresholds for charitable help to their communities.

An October 2023 report released today by Sen. Bernie Sanders (I-Vt.), chairman of the Senate Health, Education, Labor, and Pensions (HELP) Committee, shows that many nonprofit hospital systems across the country are failing to provide low-income Americans with the affordable medical care required by their nonprofit status—despite receiving billions in tax benefits and providing exorbitant compensation packages to their senior executives.

"In 2020, nonprofit hospitals received $28 billion in tax breaks for the purpose of providing affordable health care for low-income Americans," said Chairman Sanders. "And yet, despite these massive tax breaks, most nonprofit hospitals are actually reducing the amount of charity care they provide to low-income families even as CEO pay is soaring. That is absolutely unacceptable. At a time when 85 million Americans are uninsured or underinsured, over 500,000 people go bankrupt because of medically related debt, and over 60,000 Americans die each year because they cannot afford to go to a doctor when they need to, nonprofit hospitals should be providing more charity care to those who desperately need it, not less. And if they refuse to do so, they should lose their tax-exempt status."

Nearly half of American hospitals enjoy nonprofit status, which exempts them from federal, state, and local taxation. In 2020, the country's 2,978 nonprofit hospitals received an estimated $28 billion in federal, state, and local tax benefits—an average of $9.4 million per hospital. In return for nonprofit status and millions in tax breaks each year, federal law requires nonprofit hospitals to operate for the public benefit, which includes ensuring low-income individuals receive medical care for free or at significantly reduced rates—a practice known as "charity care."

However, the HELP Committee Majority's report shows many nonprofit hospitals have gladly accepted the tax benefits that come with nonprofit status, while failing to provide affordable care to those who need it most. The report examines 16 of the largest nonprofit hospital systems in the United States. While each makes more than $3 billion in revenue annually, 12 of the 16 dedicate less than 2 percent of their total revenue to charity care, including three of the nation's five largest nonprofit hospital chains. Of those 12, six dedicate less than 1 percent of their total revenue to charity care. Meanwhile, in 2021, the most recent year for which data is available for all 16 of the hospital chains, those organizations' CEOs averaged more than $8 million in compensation and collectively made more than $140 million.

In recent years, the amount of charity care provided by nonprofit hospitals has actually declined, despite the fact that patient need, revenue, and operating profits have all increased. One study found 86 percent of nonprofit hospitals spent less on charity care than they received in tax benefits between 2011 and 2018. Those additional operating profits and reserve funds were not used to help those most in need. In fact, in the same time period, average charity care spending dropped from just $6.7 million to $6.4 million.

According to the report, many of these nonprofit hospital systems also make information about their charity care programs difficult to access, leaving many patients unaware that they may qualify for free or discounted care. Some hospitals also aggressively try to collect from charity care patients through practices that verge on extraordinary collection practices banned under the Patient Protection and Affordable Care Act. One recent study found that nonprofit hospitals in 2017 sent $2.7 billion in bills to patients who were likely eligible for charity care.

The growing interest in how tax-exempt hospitals operate—from lawmakers, the public, and the media—has coincided with a stubborn increase in consumers' medical debt. *KFF Health News* reported last year that more than 100 million Americans are saddled with medical bills they can't pay and has documented aggressive bill-collection practices by hospitals, many of them nonprofits. In 2019, Oregon passed legislation to set floors on community benefit spending largely based on each hospital's past expenditures as well as its operating profit margin. Illinois and Utah created spending requirements for hospitals based on the property taxes they would have been assessed as for-profit organizations. And a congressional committee in April heard testimony on the issue.

"States have a general interest in understanding how much is being spent on community benefit and, increasingly, understanding what those expenditures are targeted at," said Maureen Hensley-Quinn, a senior director at the National Academy for State Health Policy. "It's not a blue or red state issue. It really is across the board that we've been seeing inquiries on this." Besides providing federal, state, and local tax breaks, nonprofit status also lets hospitals benefit from tax-exempt bond financing and receive charitable contributions that are tax-deductible for the donors. Policy analysts at KFF estimated the total value of nonprofit hospitals' exemptions in 2020 at about $28 billion, much higher than the $16 billion in free or discounted services they provided through the charity care portion of their community benefits.

Federal law defines the type of services to provide and level of spending that can qualify as a community benefit but does not stipulate how much hospitals need to spend. The range of community benefit activities, reported by hospitals on IRS forms, varies considerably by organization. The spending typically includes charity care—broadly defined as free or discounted care to eligible patients. But it can also include underpayments from public health plans, as well as the costs of training medical professionals and doing research.

Hospitals also claim as community benefits the difference between what it costs to provide a service and what Medicaid pays them, known as the Medicaid shortfall. But some states and policy experts argue that the shortfall shouldn't count because higher payments from commercial insurance companies and uninsured patients paying cash cover those costs. Ge Bai, of Johns Hopkins, collaborated on a 2021 study that found for every $100 in total spending, nonprofit hospitals provided $2.30 in charity care, while for-profit hospitals provided $3.80. Another study in *Health Affairs* reported substantial growth in nonprofit hospitals' operating profits and cash reserves from 2012 to 2019 "but no corresponding increase in charity care." And an April report by the *Lown Institute*, a healthcare think tank, said more than 1,350 nonprofit hospitals have "fair share" deficits, meaning the value of their community investments fails to equal the value of their tax breaks. "With so many Americans struggling with medical debt and access to care, the need for hospitals to give back as much as they take grows stronger every day," said Vikas Saini, president of the institute. The Lown Institute does not count compensating for the Medicaid shortfall, spending on research, or training medical professionals as part of hospitals' "fair share."

Hospitals have long argued they need to charge private insurance plans higher rates to make up for the Medicaid shortfall. But a recent state report from Colorado found that, even after accounting for low Medicaid and Medicare rates, hospitals get enough from private health insurance plans to provide more charity care and community benefits than they do currently and still turn a profit. The American Hospital Association strongly disagrees with the Lown and Johns Hopkins analyses.

CHAPTER 5

Educational, Scientific, and Literary Purposes and Prevention of Cruelty to Children and Animals

5.1 Educational Purposes

p. 125. Add comments on meaning of discrimination at top of page:

    A federal judge in Oregon dismissed a lawsuit[1] challenging income tax exemption for schools under Title IX.[2] The decision was a win for Christian colleges that had joined the U.S. Department of Education (DOE) in defending their federal income tax exemption in areas where their theological convictions on LGBT issues conflicted with the anti-discrimination law that requires tax-exempt organizations follow discriminatory policies. A group of 44 current and former students at religious schools filed a class-action suit arguing that the religious exemptions were incompatible with LGBT rights and that LGBT individuals were exposed to "unsafe conditions" at religious schools. The lawsuit alleged that allowing exempt status to such schools violated the antidiscrimination rules required for their tax exemption.

    Title IX provides that "[n]o person in the United States shall, on the basis of sex, be excluded from participation in, be denied the benefits of, or be subjected to discrimination under any education program or activity receiving Federal financial assistance[.]"[3] The statute includes a religious exemption, which provides that Title IX "shall not apply to an educational institution which is controlled by a religious

---

[1]*Hunter v. U.S. Department of Education.*
[2]*Christianity Today* article "Federal Judge Tosses Challenge to Christian College Exemptions" in January 2022.
[3]20 U.S.C. § 1681(a)(3).

17

organization if the application of this subsection would not be consistent with the religious tenets of such organization[.]"

Plaintiffs are 40 LGBTQ+ people who applied to, attended, or currently attend religious colleges and universities that receive federal funding. They alleged that their schools have discriminated against them by, among other things, subjecting them to discipline—expulsion, rejecting their applications for admission, and rescinding their admissions because of their sexual orientation or gender identity. Among the schools named in the lawsuit were Bob Jones University, Baylor University, Oklahoma Baptist University, Moody Bible Institute, and Fuller Theological Seminary and citations to the Supreme Court's decision in the *Bob Jones University case*.[4]

5.5 Fostering Amateur Sports Educational Purposes

p. 141. Add new paragraph:

Athletic Support Organizations: The National Collegiate Athletic Association authorizes what are called NIL (name, image, and likeness) collectives that raise funding to provide financial support for amateur athletes. The term NIL refers to an entity that honors the names, images, and likenesses of successful football, baseball, golf, and other sports players by compensating these otherwise armature athletes for the use of their name, image, or likeness. NILs were approved for tax exemption by the IRS recently under the § 501(c)(3) rules. These entities have established models that facilitate payment to current and incoming college student athletes. They provide support for scholarships and salaries. On June 9, 2023, the IRS Office of Chief Counsel released a general legal advice memorandum (GLAM).[5] According to the GLAM, several of these organizations, commonly known as NIL collectives, claim tax-exempt status under § 501(c)(3) of the Internal Revenue Code. IRS Commissioner I Daniel Werfel and Assistant Secretary for Tax Policy Lily Batchelder endorsed a release by IRS Office of Chief Counsel of GLAM 2023-004, which concludes that certain organizations that make payments to college or incoming college student athletes for rights to their NIL are, in many cases, not eligible to have tax-exempt status.

This IRS GLAM coincides with proposed similar bipartisan legislation. *The Athlete Opportunity and Taxpayer Integrity Act*, would prohibit individuals and organizations from using a charitable tax deduction for specific contributions that compensate college or incoming college student athletes for the use of their NIL. The Act aspires to protect student athletes, uphold the integrity of college athletics, and prevent the abuse of the tax code. This legislation would achieve these objectives by denying charitable deductions for donations used to compensate college or incoming college student athletes for the use of their NIL, which would include donations to NIL collectives.[6]

---

[4]*Bob Jones University v. U.S.,* 461 U.S. 574 (1983).

[5]General Legal Advice Memo 2023-004.

[6]Legislation introduced by U.S. Sens. John Thune (R-S.D.), ranking member of the Subcommittee on Taxation and Internal Revenue Service (IRS) Oversight, and Ben Cardin (D-Md.), a member of the Subcommittee on Taxation and IRS Oversight.

"A fundamental requirement for tax-exempt status under section 501(c)(3) is that an organization must operate exclusively for a public benefit, such as a religious, charitable, scientific, or educational purpose."[7] The GLAM concludes that, "'many organizations that develop paid NIL opportunities for student athletes are not tax exempt as described in section 501(c)(3) because the private benefits they provide to student athletes are not incidental, both qualitatively and quantitatively, to any exempt purpose furthered by that activity.' We agree with this conclusion that many NIL collectives should not be granted tax exempt status."

Since the recent adoption of the National Collegiate Athletic Association's NIL rules, certain organizations, like NIL collectives, have established models that facilitate payment to current and incoming college student athletes, while claiming tax-exempt status under section 501(c)(3).

They said they appreciated the IRS's attention to this important issue through the GLAM and urge the next step be taken by adapting the GLAM's conclusions into more formal guidance, such as a revenue ruling. Individuals and organizations can make certain contributions to college or incoming college student athletes for the use of their NIL.

---

[7] General Legal Advice Memo 2023-004.

Civic Leagues and Local Associations of Employees: § (c)(4)

(c) Comparison of § 501(c)(3) and § 501(c)(4) organizations.

p.149. Insert the table below after the text of paragraph (c)

Characteristic	501(c)(3) (Public Charities)	501(c)(4)
May be organization or operated for more than insubstantial profit purposes	No	No
May restrict membership to a select group of individuals or businesses	No	No
Subject to the IRC § 4958 rules prohibiting private inurement of disqualified persons	Yes	Yes
Can engage in unlimited lobbying in furtherance of the organization's exempt purpose	No	Yes
May participate in limited political activities as long as not the primary activity of the organizations	No	Yes
May participate in limited voter registration activities	Yes	Yes
Must have a dissolution clause distributing assets to a qualified charitable purpose	Yes	No
Can endorse candidates for political office	No	Yes
Political campaign spending	No	Yes—Not primary activity

Characteristic	501(c)(3) (Public Charities)	501(c)(4)
May participate in educational advocacy activities in furtherance of the organization's exempt purpose	Yes—Insubstantial	Yes—Unlimited
Subject to excise tax on lesser of qualified political expenditures or net investment income	N/A—Political expenditures are prohibited	Yes
Donations to the organization qualify for an income tax deduction for the contributor	Yes	No[1]
Donor identity *not* disclosed on Form 990, Schedule B	Yes—Donor information disclosed only on the copy filed with the IRS	Yes—Donor information not disclosed on any Schedule B
Contributions to the organizations are subject to gift tax by the donor	No	No
Assets held in the organization are subject to inclusion in the donor's estate if there is "control" under IRC sections 2036 and 2038	Yes	Yes
An estate tax deduction is allowed after inclusion in the estate	Yes	No
Organization can self-declare exempt status with the IRS by filing notification and is not required to file for tax exemption with the IRS	No	Yes
Organization may be a supported organization of an IRC section 509(a)(3) supporting organization if it meets either the IRC section 509(a)(1) or 509(a)(2) public support test and operates for qualified charitable purposes	Yes	Yes

§ 6.2 Qualifying and Nonqualifying Civic Organizations

p.152. Add to list of rulings projects qualifying for (c)(4) exempt status:

Patagonia founder gave away the company. A September 14 article in the *New York Times* will interest practitioners with tax-exempt organization experience.[2] The headline says, "Billionaire No More: Patagonia Founder Gives Away the Company, Chouinard, of Patagonia, valued at about $3 billion, to a specially designed trust and a nonprofit organization." According to the article, "The Chouinard family has transferred their ownership. Patagonia will continue to operate as a private, for-profit B-corporation, but all the company's voting stock is now in the Patagonia

---

[1] There is an exception for charitable contributions made to volunteer firefighter organizations.

[2] News in *EO Tax Journal* 2022-172.

Purpose Trust controlled by the family." All of the nonvoting stock was donated to Holdfast Collective, a newly established Section 501(c)(4) nonprofit organization to battle climate change under the direction of the family. Funding will come from Patagonia's annual dividends, now estimated at about $100 million.

One possible reason to utilize a (c)(4), rather than a (c)(3), could be that the Holdfast Collective can advocate for causes and political candidates in addition to grant-making activities, as stated on the Patagonia website. It is also likely that another reason was that Holdfast Collective, as a (c)(3), would have been categorized as a private foundation and, as such, would not have been able to own most of the stock of a for-profit company on an ongoing basis per IRC section 4943, unless there was Newman's Own–type public benefit.

p. 154. Add to list not qualifying for (c)(4) exemption:

A civic organization that benefits private individuals or operates for profit cannot qualify as a (c)(4) organization. The following groups have failed to receive exemption:

■ *Tax and Accounting Services*—The IRS denied an application for exemption as a social welfare organization under section 501(c)(4) for two reasons: (1) failure to submit adequate information and (2) the IRS's opinion that operation of a business and tax return preparation services for qualified exempt organization was not a tax-exempt activity.[3] The rationale was such activity was normally a business activity for which market-based fees are charged. The ruling stated if such services are provided for free to poor people, that activity would possibly qualify as an exempt activity. No conclusion was reached for services provided at a reduced rate or below cost. The denial letter relied primarily on Rev. Rul. 70-535, which addresses qualification for exemption for an organization formed to provide managerial, developmental, and consultative services for low- and moderate-income housing projects for a fee. Despite the fact that the organization provided such services for low to moderate income projects was no indication that the organization's primary activity was itself charitable. The activity was not distinguishable from a commercial enterprise based upon the customer base. The business activity was conducted in a manner similar to organizations operated for profit. This means, "there was nothing charitable about the organization's activities." The fact that these services are being performed for tax-exempt corporations did not change the business nature of the activity. Importantly, the ruling indicated the applicant needed to clearly provide facts that show why and how the activities accomplish a charitable purpose.

■ The annual Community Automotive event was also not given (c)(3) tax exemption as an entity promoting social welfare but instead the IRS allowed the applicant may have qualified under (c)(7) as promoting fellowship among members.[4] The ruling also discusses the educational, social, and recreational benefits which qualified a similar organization for exemption under IRC § 501(c)(7).[5] In this earlier Revenue Ruling, the decision was based on a stipulation that the social

---

[3] PLR 202236011.
[4] Priv. Ltr. Ru. 202236011.
[5] Rev. Rul. 67-216 and Rev. Rul. 68-224.

welfare activity was social and recreational. This more recent adverse ruling was based upon the organization requesting a ruling under IRC § 501(c)(3) for which it did not qualify as substantially educational, or broadly beneficial to the public. In order to qualify for exemption, the organization must apply for exemption under the specific exemption using the proper form under which it anticipates being granted tax exempt status. The IRS does not have latitude to award exemption under a different Code section.[6] Additional entities determined to not qualify for exemption because a substantial portion to activities promoted fellowship. An organization Z (focus or subjects of concern not reported) planned shows, exhibitions, and rallies for its supporters. Its social media and website offer opportunities for members to share knowledge and to exchange memorabilia—activities deemed not to be exempt purposes. These facts indicated to the IRS it operated for a substantial nonexempt social purpose precluding exemption as a (c)(3) charitable organization.[7] What qualifies for promoting (c)(3) social welfare is a somewhat mysterious subset of what qualifies for promoting social welfare under § 501(c)(4) or perhaps in any case.

■ IRS issued final adverse determination revoking Code § 501(c)(4) org.'s exempt status where it failed to establish that it was operated exclusively for promotion of social welfare.[8] The organization's primary activities involved operating a bar and gaming for members of a related organization, and it regularly carried on business with the general public in a manner similar to organizations operated for profit.

CHAPTER 6.2 Qualifying and Nonqualifying Civic Organizations

(a) Limitation on Involvement with Political Candidates

The IRS explained its reasons for revoking a (c)(4) organization's exemption by saying, "You state on your Form 1024 that you will conduct two activities: public education and outreach and grant making. Public education and outreach programs, which you initially indicated would comprise 90% of your time, are intended to inform the general public about current issues that may impact them and to promote nonpartisan causes that will help the town. You plan to publish information in print, on the Internet, and through e-mail distributions. To ensure that you effectively identify new issues and legislation that could impact your ideals, you state that you will monitor legislation, court decisions, administrative orders, and executive actions on an on-going basis. You plan to send public officials letters and issue press releases to educate and advocate your position. In order to help inform and educate the public in a more comprehensive and effective manner, you plan to utilize direct mail as

---

[6] Rev. Proc. 2022-5.
[7] Rev. Rul. 67-139, 1967-1 C.B. 129 and Rev. Rul. 77-366, 1977-2 C.B. 193.
[8] Priv. Ltr. Rul. 202321009.

well as television and radio advertisements to advocate your positions on issues and legislation.

You indicated that you have focused on issues of government accountability and transparency, health care, and economic issues at both the federal and state level. You state you have used mail, television, and the Internet to communicate your message and you intend to continue to use these mediums to further your mission. You state you have engaged in grassroots lobbying by encouraging citizens to contact elected representatives and policy leaders who are in a position to affect government policy and the current public policy debate.

According to your Form 1024, in order to further your goals, you may also make grants to state or local organizations and other exempt organizations to increase the advocacy and legislative involvement work on behalf of such policies. You indicate this will comprise 10% of your time. However, after studying several pages of data from the entity's financial records, the IRS determined exemption should be revoked without providing a numerical tally of the portion of their spending that was devoted to electioneering." The Private Letter Ruling states, "Based on our analysis of the information you provided in connection with your application, we have determined that you are not operated exclusively for the promotion of social welfare within the meaning of § 501(c)(4) and do not qualify for tax exemption."[9]

The IRS developed a list of six situations to use to determine whether the organization described in each circumstance has expended funds for a § 527(e)(2) exempt purposes as a result of an advocacy communication on a public policy issue.[10] A § 527(e)(2) exempt purpose means "the function of influencing or attempting to influence the selection, nomination, election, or appointment of any individual to any federal, state or local public office or office in a political organization, or the election of Presidential or Vice-Presidential electors, whether or not such individual or electors are selected, nominated, elected, or appointed." All the facts and circumstances must be considered when making this determination. Factors that tend to show that an advocacy communication on a public policy issue is for a § 527(e)(2) exempt function include, but are not limited to, the following:

- The communication identifies a candidate for public office.
- The timing of the communication coincides with an electoral campaign.
- The communication targets voters in a particular election.
- The communication identifies that candidate's position on the public policy issue that is the subject of the communication.
- The position of the candidate on the public policy issue has been raised as distinguishing the candidate from others in the campaign, either in the communication itself or in other public communications.
- The communication is not part of an ongoing series of substantially similar advocacy communications by the organization on the same issue.

---

[9] Priv. Ltr. Rul. 202022009.
[10] Rev. Rul. 2004-6, 2004-1 C.B. 328.

In facts and circumstances, such as those described in the six situations, factors that tend to show that an advocacy communication on a public policy issue is not for a § 527(e)(2) exempt function include, but are not limited to, the following:

- The absence of any one or more of the factors listed previously.
- The communication identifies specific legislation, or a specific event outside the control of the organization, that the organization hopes to influence.
- The timing of the communication coincides with a specific event outside the control of the organization that the organization hopes to influence, such as a legislative vote or other major legislative action (for example, a hearing before a legislative committee on the issue that is the subject of the communication).
- The communication identifies the candidate solely as a government official who is in a position to act on the public policy issue in connection with the specific event (such as a legislator who is eligible to vote on the legislation).
- The communication identifies the candidate solely in the list of key or principal sponsors of the legislation that is the subject of the communication.

Rev. Rul. 2007-41, 2007-1 C.B. 1421, analyzed 21 situations to determine whether the § 501(c)(3) organization described in each has directly or indirectly participated in a political campaign on behalf of or in opposition to a candidate for public office. All facts and circumstances are considered when making this determination. When determining whether a communication results in political campaign intervention, key factors include the following:

- Whether the statement identifies one or more candidates for a given public office;
- Whether the statement expresses approval or disapproval for one or more candidates' positions and/or actions;
- Whether the statement is delivered close in time to the election;
- Whether the statement makes reference to voting or an election;
- Whether the issue addressed in the communication has been raised as an issue distinguishing candidates for a given office;
- Whether the communication is part of an ongoing series of communications by the organization on the same issue that are made independent of the timing of any election; and
- Whether the timing of the communication and identification of the candidate are related to a nonelectoral event such as a scheduled vote on specific legislation by an officeholder who also happens to be a candidate for public office.

A communication is particularly at risk of political campaign intervention when it makes reference to candidates or voting in a specific upcoming election. Nevertheless, the communication must still be considered in context before arriving at any conclusions. The promotion of social welfare does not include direct or indirect participation or intervention in political campaigns on behalf of or in opposition to any candidate for public office. Nor is an organization operated primarily for the promotion of social welfare if its primary activity is operating a social club for the benefit, pleasure, or recreation of its members, or is carrying on a business with the general public in a manner similar to organizations which are operated for profit.[11]

6.4 Neighborhood and Homeowner's Associations

p. 157. Add following the first sentence under the heading:

To qualify under § 501(c)(4), an organization must serve a constituency that constitutes a community rather than a limited group of individuals. Therefore, a homeowner's association is not allowed such status. The basis of the denial, as stated by the Independent Office of Appeals, is that the applicant does not qualify under § 501(c)(4) as a homeowners' association because it "does not promote the social welfare or provide a community benefit because it does not allow public access." The key issue appears to be the definition of "community" in the context of a homeowner's association.[12]

As defined by Wikipedia, a community is a social unit (a group of living things) with commonality such as place, norms, culture, religion, values, customs, or identity. Communities may share a sense of place situated in a given geographical area (e.g. a country, village, town, or neighborhood) or in virtual space through communication platforms. Durable good relations that extend beyond immediate genealogical ties also define a sense of community, important to their identity, practice, and roles in social institutions such as family, home, work, government, TV network, society, or humanity at large. Although communities are usually small relative to personal social ties, "community" may also refer to large group affiliations such as national communities, international communities, and virtual communities.

6.5 Disclosures of Nondeductibility

p.165. Update the bulleted list based on inflation adjustments:

- (c)(4) organizations are excepted or excluded if the following applies:
  - More than 90 percent of all annual dues are received from members who each pay annual dues of $119 or less in tax years beginning in 2020[13] or later, and, $124 or less for tax years beginning in 2022[14] or later.

---

[11] Treas. Reg. §1.501(c)(4)-1(a)(2)(ii).
[12] Piv. Ltr. Rul. 202226014.
[13] Rev. Proc. 2019-44.
[14] Rev. Proc. 2021-45.

CHAPTER 9

Social Clubs

9.1 Organizational Requirements and Characteristics

(a) Purpose Clause and Activities

p. 202. Add at end of introduction:

Last weekly release of Written Determinations included only two Exempt Orgs. One determination came out of EO Examinations and involved a social club. Revocation was not surprising since a social club must have members to qualify as discussed later in this chapter. Here's what the IRS wrote:

> *Our adverse determination as to your exempt status was made for the following reasons: Organizations described under IRC § 501(c)(7) are organized and operated for the pleasure and recreation of their members or other non-profitable purposes and no part of the net earnings inure to the benefit of any private shareholder. You have not established that you are organized and operated exclusively for an exempt purpose within the meaning of IRC § 501(c)(7). You have no members and your gross receipts from investments have consistently exceeded the upper limit of permitted under the 35% threshold revenue tests. As a result, you are not operating substantially for pleasure, recreation, or other non-profitable purposes.*[1]

This private ruling was unusual in that facts were redacted including the address of the local Taxpayer Advocate Office that considered the case, the entity's primary exempt activity, and the IRS gross receipts test percentages.

---

[1]Priv. tr. Rul. 202303013.

The other determination came out of EO Determinations in Cincinnati and involved a Form 8940 request for advance approval of procedures under §§ 4945(g)(1) and (g)(3). The IRS approved the submitted procedures for awarding scholarships and for awarding educational grants. The grant award procedures were in keeping with the established requirements and contained no new facts resulting in previous approvals of scholarship and educational grant procedures.[2]

---

[2]Priv. Ltr. Rul. 202303014.

CHAPTER 11

Public Charities

11.2a Donor Advised Funds

p. 259. Add before 11.3 Community Foundations:

Public charities are nonprofits that receive the majority of their support from a broad base of donors that provide for their revenue—as opposed to private foundations, which are usually created and supported by just one or two persons or a family. Donor advised funds (DAFs) instead are accounts identified with a donor or donor advisor, sponsored by a public charity, commonly created by financial institutions listed below and others, such as community foundations. The donor/donor advisory may not exercise control as they would over a private foundation. Instead, the donor/donor advisor merely has a reasonable expectation of advisory privileges as to the distribution or investment of the assets held in the account associated with their name. Due to this contrast to private foundations, DAF sponsors, (including the DAF accounts they sponsor) qualify as public charities and receive the same preferential tax treatment as working charities like schools and hospitals. More than half of America's 20 top public charities are DAF sponsors, according to Helen Flannery, Research Director for the Charity Reform Initiative and Associate Fellow at the Institute for Policy Studies (IPS).[1] The donations received by the highest earning DAF sponsors now equal about $11 billion, more than the highest earning working charity. In a prior year, IPS wrote about how DAFs had become the top recipients of charitable giving in the United States. At the time, IPS was astounded to discover that DAF sponsors made up 6 of the top 10 and 9 of the top 20 most successful public-charity fundraisers in the country. The data for 2023—the most recent year for which complete data are available—reveal that DAF sponsors make up 7 of the top 10 and 11 of the top 20 public charities in the United States.

The 20 U.S. charities receiving the most contributions in 2023 were:

---

[1]Reported on September 27, 2023.

* Fidelity Charitable Gift Fund—$15.3B
* National Philanthropic Trust— $8.6B
* Schwab Charitable Fund— $7.1B
* Vanguard Charitable Endowment Program—$4.3B
** Feeding America—$4.1B
* Silicon Valley Community Foundation—$4.0B
** United Way Worldwide—$2.8B
* American Endowment Foundation—$2.6B
** ALSAC/St, Jude Children's Hospital—$2.4B
* Morgan Stanley Global Impact Fund—$2.4B
** Salvation Army—$2.3B
** Direct Relief—$2.2B
* Goldman Sachs Philanthropy Fund—$2.1B
* Chicago Community Trust—$1.8B
** Good360—$1.7B
* American Online Giving Foundation—$1.5B
* Renaissance Charitable Foundation—$1.5B
** Goodwill Industries International—$1.4B
** The Y—$1.4B
** Stanford University—$1.4B

The assets held in U.S. DAFs have grown by 513 percent over the past 10 years—growing from $38 billion in 2011 to $234 billion in 2021. And DAFs now receive more than 22 percent of all U.S. individual charitable giving.

Donors can claim the same charitable tax deductions for their contributions to DAFs. However, because DAFs have no payout requirement, some say the money often fails to move in a timely way to charities addressing urgent needs. Of particular concern to some are DAF sponsors that are affiliated with for-profit financial corporations. Some also say these commercial DAFs provide the tax benefit to their donations contributors while actually encouraging the warehousing of charitable wealth. Fidelity Charitable Gift Fund ("Fidelity") has received the highest amount of donations in the country for the past six years.

In 2023, Fidelity continued its lead by receiving $15.3 billion—more than $11 billion more than the top program-delivering nonprofit, Feeding America. Silicon Valley Community Foundation and Chicago Community Trust are included in the above list as DAF sponsors because contributions to DAFs made up 93 percent and 97 percent, respectively, of their total incoming contributions in 2023. Some of the operating nonprofits on this list, such as the United Way and Stanford University, sponsor DAF programs as well, but they are not categorized as sponsors because their DAF programs are modest compared to their other fundraising.

It is also worth noting that DAFs may have actually done even better relative to working charities than our ranking shows. In previous years, the *Chronicle of Philanthropy* has made it easy for everyone to evaluate cash contributions by

---

'Donor-Advised Fund
"Operating Nonprofit

publishing well-researched lists of top-earning non-DAF "cause-driven" charities, but they did not do that in 2021. They compiled current rankings by pulling contribution information from the tax returns of the largest DAF sponsors in the United States, and then combining that with lists of donations to operating charities from two separate sources: Bloomberg's ranking of the top-fundraising nonprofit universities and *Forbes'* list of the top-fundraising nonuniversity charities.

The *Chronicle*'s lists only included cash donations, while *Forbes'* list includes both cash and noncash donations, and that can inflate revenue numbers, particularly for relief organizations. If *Forbes'* list had only included cash donations to Feeding America, for example, they would have slipped out of the top 20. Through the charitable tax deduction, taxpayers subsidize contributions to DAFs by up to 74 cents on the dollar. Some say money stored in DAFs should be used for current social problems.

CHAPTER 12

Private Foundations—General Concepts

§ 12.1 Why Private Foundations Are Special

EXHIBIT 12.1 Private Foundation Excise Taxes

Excise Tax	Common Name	Reported on Form	Tax Imposed On Private Foundation	Others	1st Tier Tax Rate	1st Tier Tax Comment/Description	2nd Tier Tax Rate	2nd Tier Tax Comment/Description	3rd Tier Tax Rate	3rd Tier Tax Comment/Description
Section 4940	Excise Tax on Domestic Foundation Net Investment Income	Form 990-PF	X	N/A	1.39%	Not a penalty tax - Assessed on the net investment income of operating and non-operating private foundations annually. Reported on Form 990-PF	N/A	N/A	N/A	N/A
Section 4941	Self-Dealing	Form 4720	No tax liability but must file the Form		N/A	Must report the act of self-dealing on a separately e-filed Form 4720 from the disqualified person(s) and/or manager(s)	N/A	N/A	N/A	N/A
		Form 4720		Disqualified Person(1)	10%	Of the "amount involved" for each type of self-dealing transaction, for each year the transaction remailed outstanding until it is corrected.	200%	If not corrected	100% of PF assets or the aggregate tax benefits resulting from section 501(c)(3) status	Any of the penalty taxes under chapter 42 IRC sections 4941 - 4945, if repeated and willful acts or failures to act, may result in the IRS revoking the private foundation's status. This can trigger the termination tax under IRC
		Form 4720		Foundation Manager (2)	5% (max of $20K)	If the manager acted with knowledge, the "amount involved" for each type of self-dealing transaction, is additive for each year the transaction remains outstanding until it is corrected. Managers are jointly and severally are liable; and can agree to allocate among theselves.	50%	If manager refuses to agree to part of all of correction. (Max $20K)		

Section		Form		Initial Tax	Description	Additional Tax	Description	Notes
Section 4942	Failure to make minimum (5%) distributions of income	Form 4720	X	30%	Of the undistributed income for each year undistributed	100%	For each year income remains undistributed	section 507((a)(2)(A) and 507(c) and if not abated under IRC section 507(g), the effect is the government takes posession of all of the private foundation's assets.
Section 4943	Excess Business Holding Prohibition	Form 4720	X	10%	On the fair market value of excess holdings each year	200%	On the fair market value of the excess holdings if still held at the close of the taxable period	
Section 4944	Jeopardizing Investment Prohibition	Form 4720	X	10%	On the amount so invested for each year of the taxable period	25%	Of the amount not removed from Jeopardy	
	Foundation Manager	Form 4720		10% (Max $10K)	On the amount approved with knowledge unless not willful meets reasonable cause exception. Managers are jointly and severally liable for a maximum tax of $10K per investment	5% (Max $20K)	Of the amount on managers tho refused to agree to part of all of removal from Jeopardy	

(continued)

EXHIBIT 12.1 (*Continued*)

Excise Tax	Common Name	Reported on Form	Tax Imposed On — Private Foundation	Tax Imposed On — Others	1st Tier Tax Rate	1st Tier Tax Comment/Description	2nd Tier Tax Rate	2nd Tier Tax Comment/Description	3rd Tier Tax Rate	3rd Tier Tax Comment/Description
Section 4945	Prohibition on Taxable Expenditures	Form 4720	X		20%	Of each taxable expenditure	100%	Of uncorrected expenditure at the end of the taxable period		
		Form 4720		Foundation Manager	5%	Of each taxable expenditure for any manager who knowingly agrees to the expenditure; maximum for all managers $10K.	50%	On expenditure manager who refuses to correct all or part of taxable amount; maximum amount $20K		
Section 4948	Excise Tax on Foreign Foundation Gross Investment Income	Form 990-PF	X		4%	Not a penalty tax - Assessed on the gross investment income of foreign private foundations annually. See U.S./Foreign Country Treatis for exceptions. Reported on Form 990-PF				
Section 4960	Excise Tax on Excess Compensation to Covered Employees and Parachute Payments	Form 4720	X	Related Persons	21%	Not a penalty tax - Proportionate share of income in excess of $1M				

(1) Disqualified Persons - As defined in IRC section 4946 includes substantial contributors, IRC section 507(d)(2)(D), and foundation managers

(2) Foundation Manager - As defined in IRC section 4946(b)

12.4 Termination of Private Foundation Status

(e) Mergers, Split-Ups, and Transfers Between Foundations

p. 319. Add after first paragraph:

One must not forget the somewhat illogical words needed to understand tax compliance reporting and tax consequences of transfers between private foundations. Words from the sixth edition are reprinted here for reference due to their significance.

> The Transferred (recipient) foundation is not treated as a newly created organization. Furthermore, the transferor foundation has not terminated its private foundation status and need not have notified the IRS in advance of its intentions. When 25 percent or more of a foundation's assets are transferred (called a "significant disposition of assets") to one or more other private foundations, the recipient private foundation(s) "shall be treated as possessing those attributes and characteristics of the transferor which are described in [Reg. §§ 1.507-3(a)(2), (3), and (4)]." When assets are distributed to commonly controlled foundations, the transferee foundations succeed to certain other tax attributes of the transfer, in the proportion of assets received, if they are effectively controlled by the transferor.
>
> The most recent IRS private ruling on September 20, 2020, continues to issue guidance and conclusion to that stipulated in § 12.4.[1]

p. 320. Add new private letter ruling to the end of footnote 96:

Priv. Ltr. Rul. 202017026.

(h) Notifying the IRS

p. 334. Add at end of page:

The IRS revenue procedures announcing areas in which its various divisions will not issue letter rulings or determination letters, including the Associate Chief Counsel (Corporate), the Associate Chief Counsel (Financial Institutions and Products), the Associate Chief Counsel (Income Tax and Accounting), the Associate Chief Counsel (Passthroughs and Special Industries), the Associate Chief Counsel (Procedure and Administration), and the Associate Chief Counsel (Tax Exempt and Government Entities), are updated periodically.

---

[1]Rev. Proc. 2016-2 was superseded by Rev. Proc. 2017-3, which provides a revised list of areas of the Code.

CHAPTER 18

IRS Filings, Procedures, and Policies

p. 801. Add at end of introduction:

IRS Publication 78 lists organizations that qualify to receive tax-deductible contributions, as described in § 170(c) of the Internal Revenue Code. It is referred to as Pub. 78. It can be accessed on the Internet or a tax code and rulings service like CCH Standard Federal Tax Reporter (the black books). Individuals can claim an income tax deduction for donations to a charity of both cash and noncash items made to qualified organizations listed in Pub. 78. The permitted amount of the gift allowed as a tax deduction depends upon the type of charity and the donor's adjusted gross income (referred to as "AGI"). Based on the nature of property donated—cash versus stock, for example—the deduction is limited to either 30 percent or 50 percent (and up to 60 percent) of AGI as reported on the tax return, taking into account other itemized deductions and other income tax rules. Pub. 78 has guidelines spell out which types of organizations may receive tax-deductible contributions and more. Examples of charities included are community trusts, religious organization like churches, United Ways, schools, hospitals, and the many more charitable entities plus some fraternal societies qualified for tax-exempt status, among many others. Charitable giving is an important and sizable income tax deduction for some American taxpayers, so these guidelines are helpful for determining eligibility.

Pub. 78 is available in hard copy and on the Internet and lists the many organizations that have been recognized as tax exemption eligible to receive deductible donations from their supporters. The list is not all-inclusive. It does not show all organization that benefit the public—like churches or organizations exempt under a group ruling. Entities that accept donations are, however, required to issue acknowledgment receipts to their donors. An individual tax filer should request documentation for evidence their donation will be acceptable to the IRS if they examine the return. For significant amounts, a copy of the IRS determination letter—applicable ruling or determination letter indicating that contributions to it are qualified as tax-deductible—could be requested.

Pub. 78 can also be viewed in conjunction with Pubs. 561 and 526. Pub. 526 provides instructions on how to claim a deduction for charitable contributions. IRS Pub. 561 is designed to help donors determine the value of property (other than cash) that is given to qualified organizations, and what kind of information they are required to provide in order to verify the proper way the charitable contribution deduction is claimed on their tax return.

Types of NOT-IN Pub. 78 Organizations. A large number of the eligible donees are not listed in Pub. 78. The IRS states that you may deduct a charitable contribution made to, or for the use of, any of the organizations listed below that otherwise are qualified under IRC § 170(c) of the Internal Revenue Code and provides the following list:

- State or U.S. possession (or political subdivision thereof), the United States, or the District of Columbia, if made exclusively for public purposes
- An entity that is part of a group exemption
- A church, synagogue, or other religious organization
- A U.S. war veterans' organization or its post, auxiliary, trust, or foundation
- A nonprofit volunteer fire company
- A civil defense organization created under federal, state, or local
- A domestic fraternal society operating under a lodge system given for charitable purposes
- A nonprofit cemetery company if funds are irrevocably dedicated to perpetual care of the cemetery as a whole and not a particular lot or mausoleum crypt

The IRS examines a very small (less than 1 percent) portion of the 990 series returns filed each year. The National Council of Nonprofits (NCN) response to an IRS request for information to consider the current situation was not received by the IRS as possible or acceptable. The letter shares two now incontrovertible points in its response to the House Ways and Means Committee's Request for Information. As stated in the NCN letter, the

- (1) Adoption of the Form 1023-EZ in 2014 has (1) resulted in the IRS's "near abdication of its duties to protect the public by screening out unqualified or unscrupulous applicants who seek charitable tax-exempt status" and (2) precipitated "a toothless monitoring regime." This "abdication" is, in my view,[1] a serious blemish on the records of former Commissioners John Koskinen and Sunita Lough and on those at the IRS who continue what the letter calls "a meaningless tax-exempt application process."
- (2) The 2019 removal of required Schedule B donor disclosures for (c)(4)s has been another disaster, this one inflicted by the Trump administration. The failure of President Biden to reverse this blatantly partisan action makes him complicit in this violation of the public's trust in exempt organizations. As stated in the NCN letter, "it is unfortunate and troubling that the disclosure requirements for non-charitable 501(c) organizations were recently changed to provide less transparency, making it even harder for the IRS to police illegal activities." The result of the new requirements, according to the NCN letter, is (1) "secrecy undermining public trust in all nonprofit organizations," (2) "the integrity of federal, state, and local elections being questioned," and (3) an invitation to "bad actors to infiltrate and exploit the nonprofit community."

---

[1] In Paul Streckfus, editor of *EO TAX Journal's* view.

CHAPTER 24

Deductibility and Disclosures

24.1 Overview of Deductibility

p. 801. Add at end of introduction:

The IRS may revoke its determination that the organization qualifies as an organization described in § 501(c)(3) and § 170(c)(2) eligible for tax-deductible donations. Generally, the IRS will disallow deductions for contributions made to an organization on or before the date of announcement it no long qualifies appears in the Internal Revenue Bulletin. However, the IRS is precluded from disallowing a deduction if the organization has timely filed a suit for declaratory judgment under § 7428 to renew its exempt status. If the contributor (1) had knowledge of the revocation of the ruling or determination letter, (2) was aware that such revocation was imminent, or (3) was in part responsible for or was aware of the activities or omissions of the organization that brought about this revocation, deductions may be disallowed. If on the other hand a suit for declaratory judgment has been timely filed, contributions from individuals and organizations described in § 170(c)(2) that are otherwise allowable will continue to be deductible. Protection under § 7428(c) began on August 28, 2023, and would end on the date the court first determines the organization is or is not described in § 170(c)(2) as more particularly set out in § 7428(c)(1). For individual contributors, the maximum deduction protected is $1,000, with a husband and wife treated as one contributor. This benefit is not extended to any individual, in whole or in part, for the acts or omissions of the organization that were the basis for revocation.

24.6 Inflation Reduction Act

p. 825. Add at end of page.

The Inflation Reduction Act (IRA) added to tax codes in 2023 to allow state, local, and tribal governments, nonprofits, U.S. territories, rural energy co-ops, and more to access several tax credits for "Building a Clean Energy Economy." This new IRA created two new credit delivery mechanisms—elective pay also known as "direct pay" and transferability (§ 6418) that contain clean energy tax credits. It is hoped these new tools to access clean energy tax credits will be a catalyst for reaching new economic and climate goals. Secretary of the Treasury Janet L. Yellen said, "More clean energy projects will be built quickly and affordably, and more communities will benefit from the growth of the clean energy economy." This act allows tax-exempt and governmental entities to receive elective payments for 12 clean energy tax credits, including the major Investment and Production Tax credits, as well as tax credits for electric vehicles and charging stations. Businesses can also choose elective pay for three of those credits: the credits for Advanced Manufacturing (45X), Carbon Oxide Sequestration (45Q), and Clean Hydrogen (45V).

The IRA also allows businesses not using elective pay to transfer all or a portion of any of 11 clean energy credits to a third party in exchange for tax-free immediate funds so that businesses can take advantage of tax incentives if they do not have sufficient tax liability to fully utilize the credits themselves. Entities without sufficient tax liability were previously unable to realize the full value of credits, which raised costs and created challenges for financing projects. Since the bill was signed into law in 2022, the Treasury worked expeditiously to write the rules to try to keep the promised release of the legislation in the fall of 2023.

"Direct pay is a game-changer for our ability to spread the benefits of clean energy to every community in America," said John Podesta, senior advisor to the president for Clean Energy Innovation and Implementation. "This provision of the Inflation Reduction Act will make it easier for local governments, Tribes, territories, nonprofits, schools, houses of worship and more to invest in clean energy, allowing them to save money, improve public health, and better serve their communities."

The proposed regulations clarify which entities would be eligible for each credit monetization mechanism, lays out the process and timeline to claim and receive an elective payment or to transfer a credit, and addresses numerous other issues. Many of those issues were raised by stakeholders in response to the Treasury's far-reaching effort to solicit public input. The temporary regulations have an electronic pre-filing registration requirement to prevent improper payments to fraudulent actors like criminal syndicates and will provide the IRS with basic information to ensure that any taxpayer that qualifies for these credit monetization mechanisms can readily access these benefits. Seminars conducted in summer 2023 provided outreach through speaking engagements, webinars, and similar engagements.

Employment Taxes

p. 843. Add new ERC Chapter 25.4

The Employee Retention Credit (ERC or ERTC) is another tax credit for businesses and tax-exempt organizations that kept paying employees during the COVID-19 pandemic either when they were shut down due to a government order or when they had a significant decline in gross receipts during certain eligibility periods in 2020 and 2021.

The IRS announced it continues to see aggressive marketing to lure ineligible taxpayers to claim the ERC. Anyone who improperly claims the ERC must pay it back, possibly with penalties and interest. To help taxpayers avoid this, the IRS prepared a question-and-answer checklist to help figure out eligibility for the credit.

ERC Eligibility Checklist Issued by the IRS

- Did you have employees and pay wages to them between March 13, 2020, and December 31, 2021? A self-employed individual with no employees or a household employer is not eligible to claim the ERC.
- Generally, businesses and tax-exempt organizations that qualify are those that:
    - Were shut down by a government order due to the COVID-19 pandemic during 2020 or the first three calendar quarters of 2021, **or**
    - Experienced the required decline (80%) in gross receipts during the eligibility periods in 2020 or the first three calendar quarters of 2021, **or**
    - Businesses or organizations that began carrying on a trade or business after February 15, 2020, that do not need to be pandemic- or recovery-related.
- ERC can be claimed because of supply chain issues.

The IRS recommends a claimant have thorough records that show wages paid, gross receipts, government orders, and other explanatory information evidencing the economic impact of the pandemic. Its announcement explains that the ERC is complex and recommends hiring a tax professional. If one improperly claimed the ERC, the IRS says the amended return that included the ERC claim can be withdrawn, following details on its website, as long as the claim has not been processed and paid. On September 14, 2023, the IRS announced a moratorium on its own processing of newly filed ERC claims through at least December 31, 2023. The IRS also announced it was working on a settlement initiative for taxpayers who believe they shouldn't have claimed the ERC and want to study `irs.gov/ERC` for updates and repayment.

Cryptocurrency

§ 27.1 What Is Cryptocurrency?

Cryptocurrency is a digital medium of exchange that is bought, sold, and used on Internet exchanges to acquire goods and services and also as a speculative investment. Cryptocurrency is one category of digital asset. It is a "fungible token." Another category of digital asset donor and nonprofits may encounter are nonfungible tokens or NFTs. Some differences between fungible and nonfungible tokens include:

- NFTs are unique and not interchangeable. A fungible token, although traceable by unique identifiers, is considered interchangeable;
- NFTs are not ordinarily used as an alternative for fiat currency. Fungible tokens are commonly referred to as cryptocurrency precisely because they are used as a substitute for currency issued by a recognized government.
- Fungible tokens can be divided into smaller units that add up to the same value. An NFT cannot be divided although it can be co-owned.
- The IRS issued a Notice 2023-36 providing guidance on the treatment of NFT associated with collectibles under IRC section 408(m) and requesting comments. Taxpayers may rely on this notice to treat such NFT as the same type of property as the underlying collectibles.

Digital cryptocurrency "coins" or "tokens" serve as proxies for ordinary cash, such as dollars and euros, but there are no physical counterparts like bank notes or coins that can be carried around. Cryptocurrency exists only in electronic form.[1]

---

[1] Derived from Tradeleader, "What is cryptocurrency in simple words." `https://trade-leader.com/articles/cryptocurrency`.

The digital "ledger" that records all transactions is called *blockchain*. It is said to be nearly impossible to counterfeit or double-spend cryptocurrencies because blockchain is protected by cryptography.

Cryptography is "the practice and study of techniques for secure communication in the presence of adversarial behavior."[2]

Cryptocurrencies are typically independent of central banks or governments. Transactions are made and recorded on what is called a distributed accounts ledger, whose status is maintained through consensus among the operators of thousands of computers. They are theoretically immune to government interference or manipulation.[3]

§ 27.2 What Are the Various Kinds of Cryptocurrency?

The most popular cryptocurrencies right now are Bitcoin and Ethereum, but more than 10,000 different cryptocurrencies are in circulation around the world.

At least 21 million Americans own cryptocurrency.[4]

The first cryptocurrency, Bitcoin, was created in 2008 and has become a significant currency both on- and offline. Creation of the concept is attributed to "Satoshi Nakamoto," believed to be a pseudonym. Bitcoin was designed as a peer-to-peer network based on "a system for electronic transactions without relying on trust." On January 3, 2009, the Bitcoin network came into existence with Satoshi Nakamoto mining the genesis block of Bitcoin (block number 0), which had a reward of 50 Bitcoins.[5] [At this writing, that genesis block would be worth $2,844,600.]

As with most cryptocurrencies, Bitcoin runs on a blockchain (also created by Satoshi Nakamoto) or a ledger logging transactions distributed across a network of thousands of computers. The network powering Bitcoin has never been hacked. And the fundamental ideas behind cryptocurrencies help make them safe.

Today, there are thousands of cryptocurrencies.[6] These usually act as payment mechanisms but have also been developed for other uses, such as lending and borrowing or digital storage. One of the broadest uses for this technology is speculation, buying in the hope that the price will go up and the holders can make a profit. The total market capitalization of all cryptocurrencies is approximately $2 trillion.[7]

---

[2] Wikipedia, s.v. "Cryptography," last modified November 26, 2023, 18:21, `https://en.wikipedia.org/wiki/Cryptography`.

[3] Jake Frankenfield, "Cryptocurrency Explained with Pros and Cons for Investment," Investopedia, Updated November 2, 2023. `https://www.investopedia.com/terms/c/cryptocurrency.asp#citation-9`.

[4] Magda Cychowski, "Crypto fundraising 101: Beginner's guide for nonprofits," Freewill (January 14, 2023). `https://resources.freewill.com/cryptocurrency-what-nonprofits-need-to-know`.

[5] Wikipedia, s.v. "History of bitcoin," last modified December 6, 2023, 11:11 `https://en.wikipedia.org/wiki/History_of_bitcoin`.

[6] CoinMarketCap, "All Cryptocurrencies," accessed December 6, 2023. `https://coinmarketcap.com/all/views/all/`.

[7] Ibid.

According to *Forbes*,[8] the following are the top 10 cryptocurrencies based on their market capitalization with the total value of all of the coins currently in circulation, and trading values shown below:

1. Bitcoin (BTC)—Market cap: More than $821 billion

   Bitcoin's price has skyrocketed as it's become a household name. Five years ago, you could buy a Bitcoin for about $500. As of September 30, 2021, a single Bitcoin's price was more than $43,000. That's growth of about 8,600 percent. [At this writing, one Bitcoin is worth $41,722, according to `coinbase.com`.]

2. Ethereum (ETH)—Market cap: More than $266.5 billion

   Ethereum has also experienced tremendous growth. In just five years, its price went from about $11 to almost $2,217, increasing more than 20,054 percent.

3. Tether (USDT)—Market cap: More than $90.7 billion

   Unlike some other forms of cryptocurrency, Tether is a stable coin, meaning it's backed by fiat currencies like the U.S. dollar and the euro and in theory should keep its value equal to currency it tracks. The logic follows that Tether's value ought to be more consistent than other cryptocurrencies, and favored by investors who are adverse to the extreme volatility of other cryptocurrencies.

4. Binance Coin (BNB)—Market cap: More than $38.5 billion

   BNB's price in 2017 was just $0.10. By late December, 2023, it had risen to over $254, a gain of more than 253,440 percent.

5. XRP (XRP)—Market cap: More than $33.5 billion

   At the beginning of 2017, the price of XRP was $0.006. As of December 12, 2023, its price reached $0.62, equal to a rise of 10,277 percent.

6. Solana (SOL)—Market cap: More than $30.0 billion

   Launched in 2020, SOL's price started at $0.77. By December 2023 was around, $70.28, a gain of 9,027 percent.

7. USD Coin (USDC)—Market cap: More than $24.2 billion

   Like Tether, USDC is a stable coin. USDC is backed by U.S. dollars and aims for a $1 USD to 1 USDC ratio. USDC is powered by the Ethereum trading platform, and you can use USDC to complete global transactions.

8. Cardano (ADA)—Market cap: More than $21.1 billion

   In 2017, ADA's price was $0.02. As of December 12, 2023, its price was $0.60. This is an increase of more than 2,886 percent.

9. Avalance (AVAX) – Market cap: More than $14.1 billion

   Avalance distinguishes itself by delivering fast transaction speeds and low transaction fees.

10. Dogecoin (DOGE)—Market cap: More than $13.7 billion

    DOGE's price in 2017 was $0.0002. By December 12, 2023, its price was at $0.10—a 48,010 percent increase.

Source: Kat Tretina and John Schmidt, "Top Ten Cryptocurrencies," *Forbes Advisor.*

---

[8] Kat Tretina, "Top 10 Cryptocurrencies of December 2023," *Forbes Advisor,* updated December 5, 2023. `https://www.forbes.com/advisor/investing/top-10-cryptocurrencies/`.

More than 100,000 businesses accept cryptocurrency, including Expedia, Overstock, Home Depot, Whole Foods, Lowes, and Regal Cinemas. The Ohio Department of Revenue accepts digital currency, and 18 states have blockchain legislation.[9]

Many nonprofits accept and encourage cryptocurrency donations, which are the fastest growing asset donated to Fidelity Charitable. As of August 30, 2021, Fidelity Charitable has received more than $106 million in cryptocurrency donations.[10]

The IRS treats cryptocurrencies as property, and therefore cryptocurrencies are subject to general tax principles for property transactions. This means if the value of the contribution exceeds $5,000, the donor must obtain a qualified appraisal in order to take a charitable deduction.[11]

§ 27.3 Should Nonprofits Be Involved in Cryptocurrency?

The prices of cryptocurrencies like Bitcoin can rise and fall dramatically and that activity has been volatile and unpredictable. The usual advice is not to invest more than you can afford to lose. And loss is not only market based; it is possible to forget a password and completely lose an investment.

Financial advisors warn that it is critical to conduct thorough research into the complications and histories of these currencies, including understanding how blockchains work.

The following comments from an article[12] by Christopher Gordon for the Idaho Society of CPAs gives a good overview of considerations for nonprofits that are exploring cryptocurrency:

> *Why should a nonprofit organization consider accepting Bitcoin and other cryptocurrencies? Simply put: because it has value. Nonprofit organizations already accept a variety of noncash assets, including cars, boats, houses, and intellectual property. Cryptocurrency's current market valuation makes it attractive to donors to contribute for tax-planning purposes. Donors can contribute a highly appreciated asset and avoid income tax on the unrealized appreciation.*
>
> *How can we accept Bitcoin and other cryptocurrencies? There are several cryptocurrency trading platforms available today, including Coinbase and Robinhood. More are on the way, with many brokerage firms beginning to consider a cryptocurrency platform. Each platform has advantages and drawbacks so it's important to research the differences among them, including pricing and ease of use.*
>
> *What steps should we take when someone donates cryptocurrency to our nonprofit organization? The first step is proper tax reporting. A contribution of*

---

[9] U.S. Internal Revenue Service, "IRS Nationwide Tax Forum 2019." https://www.irs.gov/pub/irs-utl/2019ntf-35.pdf.

[10] Giving Block, "10 Days of Cryptocurrency Donations—#8: Fidelity Charitable Over $106 Million in Bitcoin Donations." https://thegivingblock.com/updates/news/10-days-of-cryptocurrency-donations-fidelity-charitable-raises-106-million-in-bitcoin/.

[11] IRC section 170(f)(11)(C) and 170(f)(11)(E)(i).

[12] https://www.idcpa.org/news/articles/806:cryptocurrency-considerations-for-nonprofits.

cryptocurrency valued at more than $250 requires a standard noncash dona-tion receipt. In addition, the IRS has classified cryptocurrency as property, not currency. Therefore, a donor must file Form 8283, Noncash Charitable Contri-butions, to receive a charitable deduction if the property is over $500. Further, if the contribution is valued at more than $5,000, the donor must receive a qualified appraisal prepared by a qualified appraiser to substantiate the valu-ation and the organization receiving the donation must sign Form 8283. How-ever, it is unclear if the cryptocurrency markets are sufficient to establish the valuation.

An organization that sells cryptocurrency within three years of receiving it will be required to complete Form 8282, which could impact the donor. Another feature of cryptocurrency is that sales resulting in gains are not subject to unre-lated business income.

Are there other considerations? If your organization decides to accept cryp-tocurrency, be sure to include it in your gift acceptance policy. This will guide your finance team in knowing whether to accept the transaction and the steps to take after it is received.

What if we hold cryptocurrency? What financial reporting considerations should there be? The first step is to understand where cryptocurrency should be reported on the balance sheet (statement of financial position). The Financial Accounting Standards Board (FASB) has not issued formal guidance on the ques-tion, but the topic is currently under consideration. Nonauthoritative literature has provided an analytical framework based on current FASB guidance, which excludes it from being reported as cash, a noncash financial asset (investment), or inventory because it does not meet the definition of those three classifications.

Therefore, it leaves cryptocurrency to be reported as an indefinite-lived intangible asset according to FASB ASC 360-30. Under this guidance, crypto-currency is held at cost and evaluated for other-than-temporary impairment. When material, it should be broken out onto its own line for intangible assets and disclosed.

So why shouldn't a nonprofit organization begin accepting and investing in cryptocurrency? Risk. The valuation of Bitcoin and other cryptocurrencies con-tinues to remain volatile, so the short-term fluctuations should be considered as part of your overall portfolio risk. Cryptocurrency is not a fiat currency (a cur-rency with government backing), and it could potentially turn worthless if the demand declines. It also is not an investment in a corporation creating products or services that could be evaluated and monitored.

Then there are risks related to where Bitcoin is stored. Digital wallets are only as reliable as the computer they are stored on. For example, if Bitcoin is stored in a digital wallet on a computer hard drive that becomes corrupted and is not backed up, there is a good chance the owner will not be able to retrieve the Bit-coin. Additionally, Mt. Gox was one of the most prominent Bitcoin exchanges in the world when, in 2014, all withdrawals were halted. It was speculated that the company lost hundreds of thousands of Bitcoin due to theft, which has not been uncommon with other exchanges as well.

Source: Christopher Gordon, "Cryptocurrency Considerations for Nonprof-its," Idaho Society of Certified Public Accountants (ISCPA), April 29, 2021.

§ 27.4 Cryptocurrencies and the Internal Revenue Service

The following article, by David B. Borsack of Cole Schotz P.C., is from August 2, 2021, and provides an overview of IRS views about cryptocurrency:

There are multiple regulatory schemes to be aware of when considering or pursuing opportunities within the digital asset and cryptocurrency industries beyond the various State regulations and the FinCen Rulings. There are a host of other federal agencies with their own rulings and restrictions pertaining to cryptocurrencies including the Commodity Futures Trading Commission ("CFTC"), the Internal Revenue Service ("IRS"), and the Securities and Exchange Commission ("SEC"). This article will provide a high-level overview of the IRS's stance on cryptocurrencies.

In the IRS's view, cryptocurrencies are considered to be convertible digital tokens, a virtual currency that can be exchanged for other fiat or virtual currencies. As of this writing, the IRS treats cryptocurrencies as property and therefore cryptocurrencies are subject to general tax principles for property transactions. This means that generally cryptocurrencies, including Bitcoin, are treated as a capital asset and are subject to the capital gain and loss rules.

Converting a cryptocurrency to a fiat currency, converting a cryptocurrency from one coin to another, or using a cryptocurrency to pay for goods or services are all considered to be taxable events. Accordingly, if you acquire a cryptocurrency and hold it for longer than one year, if or when you eventually dispose of it, your gain or loss will be subject to long-term capital gain rules. If you dispose of the cryptocurrency within a year of acquiring it, the gain or loss will be subject to short-term capital gain rules. The holding period to determine whether a gain or loss on the exchange or use of the cryptocurrency starts on the day after acquisition of the cryptocurrency and ends on the day you exchange or use it. An exception to this general rule of cryptocurrency being taxed as property is when a business holds cryptocurrencies to sell to customers in the ordinary course of business. Importantly, moving cryptocurrency from one wallet that you control to another is not a taxable event.

Additionally, if you are paid for goods or services that you provide in cryptocurrency, that constitutes income at the fair market value of the cryptocurrency received (as measured in U.S. dollars on the receipt date). A donation of cryptocurrency to a charity is eligible for the charitable contribution deduction and is equal to the fair market value of the cryptocurrency at the time of the donation provided you held the cryptocurrency for at least one year. If the donated cryptocurrency has been held for less than a year, the deduction is the lesser of the basis in the cryptocurrency or its fair market value at the time of the contribution. From time to time a cryptocurrency goes through a "fork," which occurs when certain miners who work on the blockchain of a specific cryptocurrency decide to implement a new protocol. Some of the miners accept the new rule, others do not, and that is how a fork occurs. Bitcoin Cash is an example of a fork from the Bitcoin blockchain. Sometimes, when a fork occurs, holders of the original cryptocurrency receive the new cryptocurrency. A receipt of a new currency from a fork is considered income, and is taxable. Below is a chart providing an overview of potential actions and whether a taxable event is created.

When determining the gain or loss on cryptocurrency, you can either specifically choose units of the currency that you sold, exchanged or used, or use the first in first out basis ("FIFO"). In order to specifically identify a unit of cryptocurrency being sold, exchanged, or used, you must show (1) the date and time each unit was acquired, (2) the basis and fair market value at the time of acquisition, (3) the date and time the unit was sold, exchanged, or used, and (4) the fair value of each unit when sold, exchanged, or used and the amount of money or value of the property received for the unit. The FIFO method results in treating the unit that sold, exchanged, or used as being the first unit of the specific cryptocurrency you acquired. This is an important distinction because it can have massive implications as to calculating the gain or loss on your cryptocurrency. For instance, assume that you acquired one Bitcoin in 2016 for $1,000, a second Bitcoin in 2019 for $10,000, and a third Bitcoin in 2020 for $25,000. You then sold one Bitcoin in 2021 for $60,000. Depending on which method you choose, your taxable income on the 2021 sale can be as high as $59,000 or as low as $35,000.

As Section 1031 like-kind exchanges are now only available for real property, 1031 transactions are not available for cryptocurrencies. At one point there was a gray area as to whether the exchange of one type of cryptocurrency for another could qualify as a 1031 transaction, but the IRS has now made it clear that a cryptocurrency exchange is not a 1031 transaction.

It is very important to be aware of how cryptocurrency is taxed if you are considering investing in the industry. Cryptocurrency is taxed as property, is subject to capital gains taxes, with a holding period determined as the day after acquisition to the day of disposition and is not eligible for Section 1031 transactions. However, any cryptocurrency that you earn is taxable as ordinary income. This includes cryptocurrencies earned through mining and cryptocurrencies acquired from the forking of a blockchain. These rules are subject to change, and it is very important to be aware of any potential changes.[13]

Source: David B. Borsack, "Cryptocurrencies and the Internal Revenue Service," Cole Schotz P.C., August 2, 2021.

IRS frequently asked questions on virtual currency[14]

Q1. What is virtual currency?

A1. Virtual currency is a digital representation of value, other than a representation of the U.S. dollar or a foreign currency ("real currency"), that functions as a unit of account, a store of value, and a medium of exchange. Some virtual currencies are convertible, which means that they have an equivalent value in real currency or act as a substitute for real currency. The IRS uses the term "virtual currency" in these FAQs to describe the

---

[13] https://www.cscorporateblog.com/2021/08/articles/crypto-currency/cryptocurrencies-and-the-internal-revenue-service/.

[14] U.S. Internal Revenue Service, "Frequently Asked Questions on Virtual Currency Transactions." https://www.irs.gov/individuals/international-taxpayers/frequently-asked-questions-on-virtual-currency-transactions.

various types of convertible virtual currency that are used as a medium of exchange, such as digital currency and cryptocurrency. Regardless of the label applied, if a particular asset has the characteristics of virtual currency, it will be treated as virtual currency for Federal income tax purposes.

Q2. *How is virtual currency treated for Federal income tax purposes?*

A2. Virtual currency is treated as property and general tax principles applicable to property transactions apply to transactions using virtual currency. For more information on the tax treatment of virtual currency, see Notice 2014-21. For more information on the tax treatment of property transactions, see Publication 544, Sales and Other Dispositions of Assets.

Q3. *What is cryptocurrency?*

A3. Cryptocurrency is a type of virtual currency that uses cryptography to secure transactions that are digitally recorded on a distributed ledger, such as a blockchain. A transaction involving cryptocurrency that is recorded on a distributed ledger is referred to as an "on-chain" transaction; a transaction that is not recorded on the distributed ledger is referred to as an "off-chain" transaction.

Q4. *Will I recognize a gain or loss when I sell my virtual currency for real currency?*

A4. Yes. When you sell virtual currency, you must recognize any capital gain or loss on the sale, subject to any limitations on the deductibility of capital losses. For more information on capital assets, capital gains, and capital losses, see Publication 544, Sales and Other Dispositions of Assets.

Q5. *The 2020 Form 1040 asks whether at any time during 2020, I received, sold, sent, exchanged, or otherwise acquired any financial interest in any virtual currency. During 2020, I purchased virtual currency with real currency and had no other virtual currency transactions during the year. Must I answer yes to the Form 1040 question?*

A5. No. If your only transactions involving virtual currency during 2020 were purchases of virtual currency with real currency, you are not required to answer yes to the Form 1040 question.

Q6. *How do I determine if my gain or loss is a short-term or long-term capital gain or loss?*

A6. If you held the virtual currency for one year or less before selling or exchanging the virtual currency, then you will have a short-term capital gain or loss. If you held the virtual currency for more than one year before selling or exchanging it, then you will have a long-term capital gain or loss. The period during which you held the virtual currency (known as the "holding period") begins on the day after you acquired the virtual currency and ends on the day you sell or exchange the virtual currency. For more information on short-term and long-term capital gains and losses, see Publication 544, Sales and Other Dispositions of Assets.

Q7. *How do I calculate my gain or loss when I sell virtual currency for real currency?*

A7. Your gain or loss will be the difference between your adjusted basis in the virtual currency and the amount you received in exchange for the virtual currency, which you should report on your Federal income tax return in U.S. dollars. For more information on gain or loss from sales or exchanges, see Publication 544, Sales and Other Dispositions of Assets.

Q8. *How do I determine my basis in virtual currency I purchased with real currency?*

A8. Your basis (also known as your "cost basis") is the amount you spent to acquire the virtual currency, including fees, commissions, and other acquisition costs in U.S. dollars. Your adjusted basis is your basis increased by certain expenditures and decreased by certain deductions or credits in U.S. dollars. For more information on basis, see Publication 551, Basis of Assets.

Q9. *Do I have income if I provide someone with a service and that person pays me with virtual currency?*

A9. Yes. When you receive property, including virtual currency, in exchange for performing services, whether or not you perform the services as an employee, you recognize ordinary income. For more information on compensation for services, see Publication 525, Taxable and Nontaxable Income.

Q10. *Does virtual currency received by an independent contractor for performing services constitute self-employment income?*

A10. Yes. Generally, self-employment income includes all gross income derived by an individual from any trade or business carried on by the individual as other than an employee. Consequently, the fair market value of virtual currency received for services performed as an independent contractor, measured in U.S. dollars as of the date of receipt, constitutes self-employment income and is subject to the self-employment tax.

Q11. *Does virtual currency paid by an employer as remuneration for services constitute wages for employment tax purposes?*

A11. Yes. Generally, the medium in which remuneration for services is paid is immaterial to the determination of whether the remuneration constitutes wages for employment tax purposes. Consequently, the fair market value of virtual currency paid as wages, measured in U.S. dollars at the date of receipt, is subject to Federal income tax withholding, Federal Insurance Contributions Act (FICA) tax, and Federal Unemployment Tax Act (FUTA) tax and must be reported on Form W-2, Wage and Tax Statement. See Publication 15 (Circular E), Employer's Tax Guide PDF, for information on the withholding, depositing, reporting, and paying of employment taxes.

Q12. How do I calculate my income if I provide a service and receive payment in virtual currency?

A12. The amount of income you must recognize is the fair market value of the virtual currency, in U.S. dollars, when received. In an on-chain transaction you receive the virtual currency on the date and at the time the transaction is recorded on the distributed ledger.

Q13. How do I determine my basis in virtual currency I receive for services I've provided?

A13. If, as part of an arm's length transaction, you provided someone with services and received virtual currency in exchange, your basis in that virtual currency is the fair market value of the virtual currency, in U.S. dollars, when the virtual currency is received. For more information on basis, see Publication 551, Basis of Assets.

Q14. Will I recognize a gain or loss if I pay someone with virtual currency for providing me with a service?

A14. Yes. If you pay for a service using virtual currency that you hold as a capital asset, then you have exchanged a capital asset for that service and will have a capital gain or loss. For more information on capital gains and capital losses, see Publication 544, Sales and Other Dispositions of Assets.

Q15. How do I calculate my gain or loss when I pay for services using virtual currency?

A15. Your gain or loss is the difference between the fair market value of the services you received and your adjusted basis in the virtual currency exchanged. For more information on gain or loss from sales or exchanges, see Publication 544, Sales and Other Dispositions of Assets.

Q16. Will I recognize a gain or loss if I exchange my virtual currency for other property?

A16. Yes. If you exchange virtual currency held as a capital asset for other property, including for goods or for another virtual currency, you will recognize a capital gain or loss. For more information on capital gains and capital losses, see Publication 544, Sales and Other Dispositions of Assets.

Q17. How do I calculate my gain or loss when I exchange my virtual currency for other property?

A17. Your gain or loss is the difference between the fair market value of the property you received and your adjusted basis in the virtual currency exchanged. For more information on gain or loss from sales or exchanges, see Publication 544, Sales and Other Dispositions of Assets.

Q18. How do I determine my basis in property I've received in exchange for virtual currency?

A18. If, as part of an arm's length transaction, you transferred virtual currency to someone and received other property in exchange, your basis in that property is its fair market value at the time of the exchange. For more information on basis, see Publication 551, Basis of Assets.

Q19. Will I recognize a gain or loss if I sell or exchange property (other than U.S. dollars) for virtual currency?

A19. Yes. If you transfer property held as a capital asset in exchange for virtual currency, you will recognize a capital gain or loss. If you transfer property that is not a capital asset in exchange for virtual currency, you will recognize an ordinary gain or loss. For more information on gains and losses, see Publication 544, Sales and Other Dispositions of Assets.

Q20. How do I calculate my gain or loss when I exchange property for virtual currency?

A20. Your gain or loss is the difference between the fair market value of the virtual currency when received (in general, when the transaction is recorded on the distributed ledger) and your adjusted basis in the property exchanged. For more information on gain or loss from sales or exchanges, see Publication 544, Sales and Other Dispositions of Assets.

Q21. How do I determine my basis in virtual currency that I have received in exchange for property?

A21. If, as part of an arm's length transaction, you transferred property to someone and received virtual currency in exchange, your basis in that virtual currency is the fair market value of the virtual currency, in U.S. dollars, when the virtual currency is received. For more information on basis, see Publication 551, Basis of Assets.

Q22. One of my cryptocurrencies went through a hard fork but I did not receive any new cryptocurrency. Do I have income?

A22. A hard fork occurs when a cryptocurrency undergoes a protocol change resulting in a permanent diversion from the legacy distributed ledger. This may result in the creation of a new cryptocurrency on a new distributed ledger in addition to the legacy cryptocurrency on the legacy distributed ledger. If your cryptocurrency went through a hard fork, but you did not receive any new cryptocurrency, whether through an airdrop (a distribution of cryptocurrency to multiple taxpayers' distributed ledger addresses) or some other kind of transfer, you don't have taxable income.

Q23. One of my cryptocurrencies went through a hard fork followed by an airdrop and I received new cryptocurrency. Do I have income?

A23. If a hard fork is followed by an airdrop and you receive new cryptocurrency, you will have taxable income in the taxable year you receive that cryptocurrency.

Q24. How do I calculate my income from cryptocurrency I received following a hard fork?

A24. When you receive cryptocurrency from an airdrop following a hard fork, you will have ordinary income equal to the fair market value of the new cryptocurrency when it is received, which is when the transaction is recorded on the distributed ledger, provided you have dominion and control over the cryptocurrency so that you can transfer, sell, exchange, or otherwise dispose of the cryptocurrency.

Q25. *How do I determine my basis in cryptocurrency I received following a hard fork?*

A25. If you receive cryptocurrency from an airdrop following a hard fork, your basis in that cryptocurrency is equal to the amount you included in income on your Federal income tax return. The amount included in income is the fair market value of the cryptocurrency when you received it. You have received the cryptocurrency when you can transfer, sell, exchange, or otherwise dispose of it, which is generally the date and time the airdrop is recorded on the distributed ledger. See Rev. Rul. 2019-24 PDF. For more information on basis, see Publication 551, Basis of Assets.

Q26. *I received cryptocurrency through a platform for trading cryptocurrency; that is, through a cryptocurrency exchange. How do I determine the cryptocurrency's fair market value at the time of receipt?*

A26. If you receive cryptocurrency in a transaction facilitated by a cryptocurrency exchange, the value of the cryptocurrency is the amount that is recorded by the cryptocurrency exchange for that transaction in U.S. dollars. If the transaction is facilitated by a centralized or decentralized cryptocurrency exchange but is not recorded on a distributed ledger or is otherwise an off-chain transaction, then the fair market value is the amount the cryptocurrency was trading for on the exchange at the date and time the transaction would have been recorded on the ledger if it had been an on-chain transaction.

Q27. *I received cryptocurrency in a peer-to-peer transaction or some other type of transaction that did not involve a cryptocurrency exchange. How do I determine the cryptocurrency's fair market value at the time of receipt?*

A27. If you receive cryptocurrency in a peer-to-peer transaction or some other transaction not facilitated by a cryptocurrency exchange, the fair market value of the cryptocurrency is determined as of the date and time the transaction is recorded on the distributed ledger, or would have been recorded on the ledger if it had been an on-chain transaction. The IRS will accept as evidence of fair market value the value as determined by a cryptocurrency or blockchain explorer that analyzes worldwide indices of a cryptocurrency and calculates the value of the cryptocurrency at an exact date and time. If you do not use an explorer value, you must establish that the value you used is an accurate representation of the cryptocurrency's fair market value.

Q28. *I received cryptocurrency that does not have a published value in exchange for property or services. How do I determine the cryptocurrency's fair market value?*

A28. When you receive cryptocurrency in exchange for property or services, and that cryptocurrency is not traded on any cryptocurrency exchange and does not have a published value, then the fair market value of the cryptocurrency received is equal to the fair market value of the property or services exchanged for the cryptocurrency when the transaction occurs.

Q29. When does my holding period start for cryptocurrency I receive?

A29. Your holding period begins the day after it is received. For more information on holding periods, see Publication 544, Sales and Other Dispositions of Assets.

Q30. Do I have income when a soft fork of cryptocurrency I own occurs?

A30. No. A soft fork occurs when a distributed ledger undergoes a protocol change that does not result in a diversion of the ledger and thus does not result in the creation of a new cryptocurrency. Because soft forks do not result in you receiving new cryptocurrency, you will be in the same position you were in prior to the soft fork, meaning that the soft fork will not result in any income to you.

Q31. I received virtual currency as a bona fide gift. Do I have income?

A31. No. If you receive virtual currency as a bona fide gift, you will not recognize income until you sell, exchange, or otherwise dispose of that virtual currency. For more information about gifts, see Publication 559, Survivors, Executors, and Administrators.

Q32. How do I determine my basis in virtual currency that I received as a bona fide gift?

A32. Your basis in virtual currency received as a bona fide gift differs depending on whether you will have a gain or a loss when you sell or dispose of it. For purposes of determining whether you have a gain, your basis is equal to the donor's basis, plus any gift tax the donor paid on the gift. For purposes of determining whether you have a loss, your basis is equal to the lesser of the donor's basis or the fair market value of the virtual currency at the time you received the gift. If you do not have any documentation to substantiate the donor's basis, then your basis is zero. For more information on basis of property received as a gift, see Publication 551, Basis of Assets.

Q33. What is my holding period for virtual currency that I received as a gift?

A33. Your holding period in virtual currency received as a gift includes the time that the virtual currency was held by the person from whom you received the gift. However, if you do not have documentation substantiating that person's holding period, then your holding period begins the day after you receive the gift. For more information on holding periods, see Publication 544, Sales and Other Dispositions of Assets.

Q34. If I donate virtual currency to a charity, will I have to recognize income, gain, or loss?

A34. If you donate virtual currency to a charitable organization described in Internal Revenue Code Section 170(c), you will not recognize income, gain, or loss from the donation. For more information on charitable contributions, see Publication 526, Charitable Contributions.

Q35. How do I calculate my charitable contribution deduction when I donate virtual currency?

A35. Your charitable contribution deduction is generally equal to the fair market value of the virtual currency at the time of the donation if you have held the virtual currency for more than one year. If you have held the virtual currency for one year or less at the time of the donation, your deduction is the lesser of your basis in the virtual currency or the virtual currency's fair market value at the time of the contribution. For more information on charitable contribution deductions, see Publication 526, Charitable Contributions.

Q36. *When my charitable organization accepts virtual currency donations, what are my donor acknowledgment responsibilities?*

A36. A charitable organization can assist a donor by providing the contemporaneous written acknowledgment that the donor must obtain if claiming a deduction of $250 or more for the virtual currency donation. See Publication 1771, Charitable Contributions Substantiation and Disclosure Requirements PDF, for more information.

A charitable organization is generally required to sign the donor's Form 8283, Noncash Charitable Contributions, acknowledging receipt of charitable deduction property if the donor is claiming a deduction of more than $5,000 and if the donor presents the Form 8283 to the organization for signature to substantiate the tax deduction. The signature of the donee on Form 8283 does not represent concurrence in the appraised value of the contributed property. The signature represents acknowledgement of receipt of the property described in Form 8283 on the date specified and that the donee understands the information reporting requirements imposed by section 6050L on dispositions of the donated property (see discussion of Form 8282 in FAQ 36). See Form 8283 instructions for more information. (12/2019)

Q37. *When my charitable organization accepts virtual currency donations, what are my IRS reporting requirements?*

A37. Charitable organization that receives virtual currency should treat the donation as a noncash contribution. See Publication 526, Charitable Contributions, for more information. Tax-exempt charity responsibilities include the following:

Charities report noncash contributions on a Form 990-series annual return and its associated Schedule M, if applicable. Refer to the Form 990 and Schedule M instructions for more information.

Charities must file Form 8282, Donee Information Return, if they sell, exchange or otherwise dispose of charitable deduction property (or any portion thereof)—such as the sale of virtual currency for real currency as described in FAQ #4—within three years after the date they originally received the property and give the original donor a copy of the form. See the instructions on Form 8282 for more information.

Q38. *Will I have to recognize income, gain, or loss if I own multiple digital wallets, accounts, or addresses capable of holding virtual currency and transfer my virtual currency from one to another?*

A38. No. If you transfer virtual currency from a wallet, address, or account belonging to you, to another wallet, address, or account that also belongs to you, then the transfer is a non-taxable event, even if you receive an information return from an exchange or platform as a result of the transfer.

Q39. *I own multiple units of one kind of virtual currency, some of which were acquired at different times and have different basis amounts. If I sell, exchange, or otherwise dispose of some units of that virtual currency, can I choose which units are deemed sold, exchanged, or otherwise disposed of?*

A39. Yes. You may choose which units of virtual currency are deemed to be sold, exchanged, or otherwise disposed of if you can specifically identify which unit or units of virtual currency are involved in the transaction and substantiate your basis in those units.

Q40. *How do I identify a specific unit of virtual currency?*

A40. You may identify a specific unit of virtual currency either by documenting the specific unit's unique digital identifier such as a private key, public key, and address, or by records showing the transaction information for all units of a specific virtual currency, such as Bitcoin, held in a single account, wallet, or address. This information must show (1) the date and time each unit was acquired, (2) your basis and the fair market value of each unit at the time it was acquired, (3) the date and time each unit was sold, exchanged, or otherwise disposed of, and (4) the fair market value of each unit when sold, exchanged, or disposed of, and the amount of money or the value of property received for each unit.

Q41. *How do I account for a sale, exchange, or other disposition of units of virtual currency if I do not specifically identify the units?*

A41. If you do not identify specific units of virtual currency, the units are deemed to have been sold, exchanged, or otherwise disposed of in chronological order beginning with the earliest unit of the virtual currency you purchased or acquired; that is, on a first in, first out (FIFO) basis.

Q42. *If I engage in a transaction involving virtual currency but do not receive a payee statement or information return such as a Form W-2 or Form 1099, when must I report my income, gain, or loss on my Federal income tax return?*

A42. You must report income, gain, or loss from all taxable transactions involving virtual currency on your Federal income tax return for the taxable year of the transaction, regardless of the amount or whether you receive a payee statement or information return.

Q43. *Where do I report my capital gain or loss from virtual currency?*

A43. You must report most sales and other capital transactions and calculate capital gain or loss in accordance with IRS forms and instructions, including on Form 8949, Sales and Other Dispositions of Capital Assets, and then summarize capital gains and deductible capital losses on Form 1040, Schedule D, Capital Gains and Losses.

Q44. *Where do I report my ordinary income from virtual currency?*

A44. You must report ordinary income from virtual currency on Form 1040, U.S. Individual Tax Return, Form 1040-SS, Form 1040-NR, or Form 1040,

Schedule 1, Additional Income and Adjustments to Income PDF, as applicable.

Q45. Where can I find more information about the tax treatment of virtual currency?

A45. Information on virtual currency is available at Virtual Currencies (`IRS.gov/virtual_currency`). Many questions about the tax treatment of virtual currency can be answered by referring to Notice 2014-21 PDF and Rev. Rul. 2019-24 PDF.

Q46. What records do I need to maintain regarding my transactions in virtual currency?

A46. The Internal Revenue Code and regulations require taxpayers to maintain records that are sufficient to establish the positions taken on tax returns. You should therefore maintain, for example, records documenting receipts, sales, exchanges, or other dispositions of virtual currency and the fair market value of the virtual currency.

Source: Frequently Asked Questions on Virtual Currency Transactions, Notice 2014-21.

Table of Cases

Table of IRS Revenue Rulings

Revenue Rulings	Sections
54-394, 1954-2 C.B. 131	§6.2
55-70, 1955-1 C.B. 506	§24.3(b)
55-230, 1955-1 C.B. 71	§7.2(a)
55-311, 1955-1 C.B. 72	§6.2
55-319, 1955-1 C.B. 119	§10.3(f)
55-406, 1955-1 C.B. 73	§4.1
55-449, 1955-2 C.B. 599	§21.8(g)
55-587, 1955-2 C.B. 261	§5.1(e)
55-676, 1955-2 C.B. 266	§21.7(c)
56-84, 1956-1 C.B. 201	§8.4(b)
56-138, 1956-1 C.B. 202	§4.1
56-185, 1956-1 C.B. 202	§4.6(a)
56-245, 1956-1 C.B. 204	§7.2(a)
56-299, 1965-2 C.B. 165	§4.1
56-305, 1956-2 C.B. 307	§9.1(b)
56-403, 1956-2 C.B. 307	§§2.2(a), 4.5
57-128, 1957-1 C.B. 311	§§10.3(e), 10.3(f)
57-574, 1957-2 C.B. 161	§3.4
58-224, 1958-1 C.B. 242	§8.4(b)
58-293, 1958-1 C.B. 146	§8.11
58-294, 1958-1 C.B. 244	§8.3(b)
58-501, 1958-2 C.B. 262	§§9.2, 9.2(b)
58-588, 1958-2 C.B. 265	§9.3(b)
58-589, 1958-2 C.B. 266	§§9.1(a), 9.2(a), 9.3
59-6, 1959-1 C.B. 121	§7.1(b)
59-129, 1959-1 C.B. 58	§3.2(b)
59-234, 1959-2 C.B. 149	§§8.4(b), 20.8(b)
59-373, 1959-2 C.B. 37	§10.3(d)
59-391, 1959-2 C.B. 159	§8.3
60-34, 1960-2 C.B. 172	§10.3(e)
60-86, 1960-1 C.B. 198	§7.2
60-106, 1969-1 C.B. 153	§20.8(c)
60-143, 1970-1 C.B. 192	§21.7(c)
60-384, 1960-2 C.B. 172	§§10.2, 10.3(c), 10.3(e), 10.3(f)
61-87, 1961-1 C.B. 191	§4.5
61-170, 1961-2 C.B. 112	§8.4(b)
61-177, 1961-2 C.B. 117	§§8.2, 8.4(a), 8.9, 23.1(a), 23.6
61-181, 1961-2 C.B. 21	§10.3(d)
62-17, 1962-1 C.B. 87	§7.1(b)
62-23, 1962-1 C.B. 200	§5.1(a)
62-113, 1962-2 C.B. 109	§2.2(a)

Revenue Rulings	Sections
62-167, 1962-2 C.B. 142	§6.2
62-191, 1962-2 C.B. 146	§7.1(b)
63-73, 1963-1 C.B. 35	§24.1(c)
63-156, 1963-2 C.B. 79	§25.2(a)
63-190, 1963-2 C.B. 212	§§9.1(b), 9.2(b)
63-220, 1963-2 C.B. 208	§4.5
63-235, 1963-2 C.B. 210	§4.5
64-118, 1964-1 C.B. 182	§§5.1(f), 5.1(g), 9.1(b)
64-174, 1964-1 C.B. 183	§5.1(g)
64-182, 1964-1 C.B. 186	§§2.2(d), 2.2(e)
64-187, 1964-1 C.B. 354	§6.2
64-195, 1964-2 C.B. 138	§23.4(a)
64-274, 1964-2 C.B. 141	§5.1(a)
65-1, 1965-1 C.B. 226	§5.3(a)
65-14, 1965-1 C.B. 236	§8.4(b)
65-61, 1965-1 C.B. 234	§5.4
65-64, 1965-1 C.B. 241	§9.2(b)
65-164, 1965-1 C.B. 238	§8.4(a)
65-195, 1965-2 C.B. 164	§6.2
65-244, 1965-2 C.B. 167	§20.8(c)
65-270, 1965-2 C.B. 160	§5.1(e)
65-271, 1965-2 C.B. 161	§5.1(g)
65-298, 1965-2 C.B. 163	§§4.5, 5.1(e), 5.3(a)
65-299, 1965-2 C.B. 165	§6.2
66-59, 1966-1 C.B. 142	§6.3(b)
66-79, 1966-1 C.B. 48	§§8.11, 24.1(c)
66-97	§13.2(a)
66-102, 1966-1 C.B. 133	§10.4(b)
66-103, 1866-1 C.B. 134	§4.5
66-105, 1966-1 C.B. 145	§7.2(b)
66-147, 1966-1 C.B. 137	§§5.1(j), 5.3, 5.3(a)
66-150, 1966-1 C.B. 147	§§9.1(b), 10.4(a)
66-151, 1966-1 C.B. 152	§8.7
66-177, 1966-1 C.B. 132	§13.6
66-178, 1966-1 C.B. 138	§5.1(h)
66-179, 1966-1 C.B. 139	§§6.2, 7.3, 8.3(c), 9.1(b)
66-223, 1966-2 C.B. 224	§8.4(a)
66-295, 1966-2 C.B. 207	§10.4(a)
66-338, 1966-2 C.B. 226	§20.8(c)
66-354, 1966-2 C.B. 207	§7.1(c)
66-358, 1966-2 C.B. 216	§24.3(a)

Revenue Rulings	Sections	Revenue Rulings	Sections
66-359, 1966-2 C.B. 219	§5.6	68-639, 1968-2 C.B. 220	§9.2
67-4, 1967-1 C.B. 121	§§4.5, 5.1(j)	68-655, 1968-2 C.B. 613	§4.2
67-6, 1967-1 C.B. 135	§§6.4, 23.4(a)	69-68, 1969-1 C.B. 153	§9.1(b)
67-7, 1967-1 C.B. 137	§7.1(b)	69-106, 1969-1 C.B. 153	§8.4(a)
67-8, 1967-1 C.B. 142	§§2.2(a), 9.1(b)	69-174, 1969-1 C.B. 149	§4.1
67-26, 1967-2 C.B. 104	§24.2(e)	69-175, 1969-1 C.B. 149	§20.8(b)
67-71, 1967-1 C.B. 125	§23.2(c)	69-256, 1969-1 C.B. 151	§2.2(a)
67-77, 1967-1 C.B. 138	§8.3(b)	69-257, 1969-1 C.B. 151	§4.5
67-138, 1967-1 C.B. 129	§4.2	69-266, 1969-1 C.B. 151	§20.7
67-139, 1967-1 C.B. 129	§9.1(b)	69-279, 1969-1 C.B. 152	§§2.1(d), 2.2(a)
67-148, 1967-1 C.B. 132	§5.1(e)	69-381, 1969-2 C.B. 113	§10.4(a)
67-150, 1967-1 C.B. 133	§4.1	69-383, 1969-2 C.B. 113	§§4.6(b), 20.3(b)
67-151, 1967-1 C.B. 134	§5.6	69-384, 1969-2 C.B. 112	§6.2
67-176, 1967-1 C.B. 140	§8.4(b)	69-386, 1969-2 C.B. 123	§7.1(c)
67-217, 1967-2 C.B. 181	§§4.5, 5.1(a)	69-441, 1969-2 C.B. 115	§4.1
67-246, 1967-2 C.B. 104	§§24.1(a), 24.2(e)	69-464, 1969-2 C.B. 132	§21.12(a)
67-250, 1967-2 C.B. 182	§4.2	69-526, 1969-2 C.B. 115	§5.3(a)
67-251, 1967-2 C.B. 196	§§7.2(b), 8.7	69-527, 1969-2 C.B. 125	§9.1(b)
67-252, 1967-2 C.B. 195	§7.2(b)	69-528, 1969-2 C.B. 127	§§10.4(a), 21.4(b), 21.8(b)
67-284, 1967-2 C.B. 55	§21.9(f)		
67-290, 1967-2 C.B. 183	§10.3(e)	69-545, 1969-2 C.B. 117	§§4.6(a), 4.6(e)
67-292, 1967-2 C.B. 184	§§4.2, 5.1(h)	69-635, 1969-2 C.B. 126	§§9.1(a), 9.1(b)
67-293, 1967-2 C.B. 185	§23.4(a)	70-31, 1970-1 C.B. 130	§8.6
67-294, 1967-2 C.B. 193	§6.2	70-32, 1970-1 C.B. 140	§9.1(b)
67-295, 1967-2 C.B. 197	§8.4(b)	70-47, 1970-1 C.B. 49	§24.3(b)
67-325, 1967-2 C.B. 113	§4.6(g)	70-48, 1970-1 C.B. 133	§9.2
67-368, 1967-2 C.B. 194	§6.0	70-79, 1970-1 C.B. 127	§2.2(j)
67-392, 1967-2 C.B. 191	§§5.1(e), 5.1(g)	70-81, 1970-1 C.B. 131	§8.8
67-428, 1967-2 C.B. 204	§9.3(b)	70-95, 1970-1 C.B. 137	§8.4(b)
68-14, 1968-1 C.B. 243	§6.2	70-129, 1970-1 C.B. 128	§5.3(a)
68-15, 1968-1 C.B. 244	§4.2	70-186, 1970-1 C.B. 128	§4.2
68-68, 1968-1 C.B. 51	§25.2(a)	70-187, 1970-1 C.B. 131	§8.4(a)
68-70, 1968-1 C.B. 248	§4.2	70-321, 1970-1 C.B. 129	§23.2(b)
68-72, 1968-1 C.B. 250	§3.1(c)	70-344	§13.2(a)
68-118, 1968-1 C.B. 261	§6.2	70-372, 1970-2 C.B. 118	§7.2(b)
68-165, 1968-1 C.B. 253	§§5.1(e), 17.5	70-533, 1970-2 C.B. 112	§§4.1, 5.1(a), 5.1(c)
68-168, 1968-1 C.B. 269	§§9.1(b), 9.2(b)	70-534, 1970-2 C.B. 113	§§5.1(e), 21.14
68-182, 1968-1 C.B. 263	§8.3(b)	70-583, 1970-2 C.B. 114	§4.1
68-222, 1968-1 C.B. 243	§10.4(a)	70-585, 1970-2 C.B. 115	§§4.1, 4.2(a), 21.8(g)
68-224, 1968-1 C.B. 222	§6.2	70-591, 1970-2 C.B. 118	§8.4(b)
68-264, 1968-1 C.B. 264	§8.4	70-641, 1970-2 C.B. 119	§§8.3, 8.9
68-265, 1968-1 C.B. 265	§8.4(b)	71-29, 1971-_ C.B. 150	§4.3
68-306, 1968-1 C.B. 257	§3.1(b)	71-97, 1971-1 C.B. 150	§4.5
68-307, 1968-1 C.B. 258	§5.1(j)	71-99, 1971-1 C.B. 151	§4.3
68-371, 1968-2 C.B. 204	§§10.4, 10.4(c)	71-131, 1971-1 C.B. 28	§10.3(b)
68-372, 1968-2 C.B. 205	§5.1(h)	71-132, 1971-1 C.B. 29	§10.3(b)
68-373, 1968-2 C.B. 206	§§5.3(a), 5.4	71-155, 1971-1 C.B. 152	§8.4(b)
68-432, 1968-2 C.B. 104	§§24.3(a), 24.3(b)	71-311, 1971-2 C.B.	§21.12(b)
68-438, 1968-2 C.B. 609	§4.2	71-395, 1971-2 C.B. 228	§§5.1(h), 20.8(b)
68-504, 1968-2 C.B. 211	§§5.1(e), 21.8(b)	71-421, 1971-2 C.B. 229	§9.1(b)
68-534, 1968-2 C.B. 217	§7.1(b)	71-447, 1971-2 C.B. 230	§17.3(d)
68-535, 1968-2 C.B. 219	§9.2(b)	71-504, 1971-2 C.B. 231	§§8.2, 8.4(a), 8.11
68-563, 1968-2 C.B. 212	§3.1(c)	71-505, 1971-2. C.B. 232	§8.11
68-609, 1968-2 C.B. 227	§20.7	71-506, 1971-2 C.B. 233	§8.11

Revenue Rulings	Sections	Revenue Rulings	Sections
71-529, 1971-2 C.B. 234	§21.8(b)	74-197, 1974-1 C.B. 143	§21.12(b)
71-544, 1971-2 C.B. 227	§10.4(a)	74-224, 1974-1 C.B. 61	§3.2(c)
71-545, 1971-2 C.B. 235	§5.1(h)	74-246, 1974-1 C.B. 130	§4.3
71-580	§21.7(a)	74-281, 1979-1 C.B. 133	§6.3(a)
72-102, 1972-1 C.B. 149	§6.4	74-287, 1974-1 C.B. 327	§12.2(c)
72-124, 1972-1 C.B. 145	§4.6(i)	74-308, 1974-2 C.B. 168	§8.4(b)
72-147, 1972-1 C.B. 147	§20.8(b)	74-361, 1974-2 C.B. 159	§§4.3, 6.2
72-228, 1972-1 C.B. 148	§4.2	74-399 1974-2 C.B.172	§21.9(c)
72-369, 1972-2 C.B. 245	§21.8(b)	74-403, 1974-2 C.B. 381	§13.2(a)
72-391, 1972-2 C.B. 249	§7.2(b)	74-404, 1974-2 C.B. 382	§13.2(b)
72-430, 1972-2 C.B. 105	§5.1(a)	74-425, 1974-2 C.B. 373	§9.1(b)
72-462, 1972-2 C.B. 76	§25.2(a)	74-450, 1974-2 C.B.388	§15.4(g)
72-512, 1972-2 C.B. 246	§23.2(b)	74-489, 1974-2 C.B. 169	§9.3(c)
72-513, 1972-2 C.B. 246	§§23.2(b), 23.4(a)	74-497, 1974-2 C.B. 383	§13.2
72-529	§21.8(b)	74-498, 1974-2 C.B. 387	§15.1(c)
72-606, 1972-2 C.B. 78	§3.2(c)	74-518, 1974-2 C.B. 166	§7.2(b)
73-104, 1973-1 C.B. 263	§21.13	74-553, 1974-2 C.B. 168	§§8.4(a), 8.11
73-105, 1973-1 C.B. 265	§21.13	74-560, 1974-2 C.B. 389	§15.4(f)
73-126, 1973-1 C.B. 220	§20.2	74-572, 1974-2 C.B. 82	§11.2(c)
73-128, 1973-1 C.B. 222	§§4.1, 4.5, 5.1(e),	74-574, 1974-2 C.B. 160	§23.2(b)
	21.7(a)	74-575, 1974-2 C.B. 161	§3.1(b)
73-285, 1973-2 C.B. 174	§4.2	74-579, 1974-2 C.B. 383	§13.4(b)
73-320, 1973-2 C.B. 385	§§13.2, 15.5(e)	74-587, 1974-2 C.B. 162	§4.2(c)
73-363, 1973-2 C.B. 383	§14.2(c)	74-595, 1974-2 C.B. 164	§5.1(e)
73-407, 1973-2 C.B. 383	§§14.5(e), 24.3(a)	74-596, 1974-2 C.B. 167	§7.1(b)
73-411, 1973-2 C.B. 180	§8.3(b)	74-600, 1974-2 C.B. 385	§14.2(c)
73-424, 1973-2 C.B. 190	§§21.6(a), 21.15(c)	74-614, 1974-2 C.B. 164	§§2.2(j), 21.8(b)
73-434, 1973-2 C.B. 71	§5.1(a)	74-625, 1974-2 C.B. 407	§21.8(b)
73-440, 1973-2 C.B. 177	§23.4(a)	75-25, 1975-1 C.B. 359	§14.1(c)
73-452, 1973-2 C.B. 183	§8.4(b)	75-38, 1975-1 C.B. 161	§§2.1(g), 12.2(a)
73-520, 1973-2 C.B. 180	§§7.2(a), 9.1(b)	75-42, 1975-1 C.B. 359	§14.5(e)
73-546, 1973-2 C.B. 384	§14.4(e)	75-65, 1975-1 C.B. 79	§24.1(c)
73-563, 1973-2 C.B. 24	§§10.2, 10.3(d)	75-74, 1975-1 C.B. 152	§4.0
73-564, 1973-2 C.B. 28	§17.3(g)	75-196, 1975-1 C.B. 155	§5.1(h)
73-567, 1973-2 C.B. 178	§§8.4(a), 8.11	75-198, 1975-1 C.B. 157	§§4.1, 22.4(c)
73-613, 1973-2 C.B. 385	§§14.5(a), 15.4(f)	75-200, 1975-1 C.B. 163	§21.6(a)
74-13, 1974-1 C.B. 14	§21.9(f)	75-201, 1975-1 C.B. 164	§21.6(a)
74-14, 1974-1 C.B. 125	§10.3(e)	75-207, 1975-1 C.B. 361	§15.1(c)
74-15, 1974-1 C.B. 126	§10.3(e)	75-283, 1975-2 C.B. 201	§4.1
74-16, 1974-1 C.B. 126	§5.1(e)	75-285, 1975-2 C.B. 203	§4.2
74-17, 1974-1 C.B. 130	§6.2	75-286, 1975-2 C.B. 210	§6.2
74-30, 1974-1 C.B. 137	§9.1(b)	75-288, 1975-2 C.B. 212	§7.1(b)
74-38, 1974-1 C.B. 144	§21.6(a)	75-359, 1975-2 C.B. 79	§10.3(f)
74-99, 1974-1 C.B. 131	§6.4	75-384, 1975-2 C.B. 204	§§4.2, 6.2
74-116, 1974-1 C.B. 127	§5.1(e)	75-387, 1975-2 C.B. 216	§11.5(c)
74-117, 1974-1 C.B. 128	§23.2(c)	75-392, 1975-2 C.B. 447	§15.1(c)
74-118, 1974-1 C.B. 134	§7.2(a)	75-393, 1975-2 C.B. 451	§17.3(a)
74-125, 1974-1 C.B. 327	§17.3(b)	75-410, 1975-2 C.B. 446	§13.4(a)
74-148, 1974-1 C.B. 138	§9.1(b)	75-435, 1975-2 C.B. 215	§§11.2(f), 13.6
74-167, 1974-1 C.B. 134	§7.1(e)	75-442, 1975-2 C.B. 448	§15.5(e)
74-168, 1974-1 C.B. 139	§9.3(c)	75-470, 1975-2 C.B. 207	§5.1(h)
74-183, 1974-1 C.B. 328	§13.6	75-471, 1975-2 C.B. 207	§5.1(g)
74-194, 1974-1 C.B. 129	§5.6	75-473, 1975-2 C.B. 213	§7.1(b)
74-195, 1974-1 C.B. 135	§7.2(b)	75-492, 1975-2 C.B. 80	§5.1(a)

Revenue Rulings	Sections	Revenue Rulings	Sections
75-494, 1975-2 C.B. 214	§9.1(b)	77-153, 1977-1 C.B. 147	§7.2(b)
75-495, 1975-2 C.B. 44	§15.4(f)	77-154, 1977-1 C.B. 148	§§7.1(b), 7.1(e)
75-511, 1975-2 C.B. 450	§15.4(g)	77-160, 1970-1 C.B. 351	§14.5(c)
76-4, 1976-1 C.B. 145	§5.1(g)	77-164, 1977-1 C.B. 20	§§10.2, 10.3(d)
76-10, 1976-1 C.B. 355	§14.7(b)	77-165, 1977-1 C.B. 21	§§10.2, 10.3(d)
76-18, 1976-1 C.B. 355	§14.2(a)	77-206, 1977-1 C.B. 149	§8.7
76-21, 1976-1 C.B. 147	§4.1	77-213, 1977-1 C.B. 357	§17.6(d)
76-22, 1976-1 C.B. 148	§4.1	77-246, 1977-2 C.B. 190	§§2.2(j), 4.1
76-31, 1976-1 C.B. 157	§7.1(b)	77-259, 1977-2 C.B. 387	§§14.2, 14.4(e)
76-33, 1976-1 C.B. 169	§21.10(c)	77-272, 1977-2 C.B. 191	§5.1(e)
76-81, 1976-1 C.B. 156	§6.2	77-288, 1977-2 C.B. 388	§14.4(e)
76-85, 1976-1 C.B. 357	§15.1(c)	77-331, 1977-2 C.B. 388	§14.5
76-93, 1976-1 C.B. 170	§21.6(a)	77-366, 1977-2 C.B. 192	§§3.1(b), 21.14
76-94, 1976-1 C.B. 171	§21.7(a)	77-379, 1977-2 C.B. 387	§14.2(b), 14.3(a)
76-95, 1976-1 C.B. 172	§21.12(b)	77-380, 1977-2 C.B. 419	§17.3(a)
76-96, 1976-1 C.B. 23	§21.8(i)	77-429, 1977-2 C.B. 189	§10.4(b)
76-147, 1976-1 C.B. 151	§§4.2, 6.4	77-430, 1977-2 C.B. 1914	§§3.1(b), 21.14
76-152, 1976-1 C.B. 151	§§5.1(h), 20.8(b)	78-41, 1978-1 C.B. 148	§2.2(h)
76-167, 1976-1 C.B. 329	§5.1(a)	78-51, 1978-1 C.B. 165	§8.4(b)
76-204, 1976-1 C.B. 152	§4.2	78-68, 1978-1 C.B. 149	§4.3
76-207, 1976-1 C.B. 1578	§8.8	78-69, 1978-1 C.B. 156	§6.2
76-232, 1976-1 C.B.62	§24.1(a)	78-77, 1978-1 C.B. 378	§14.2(a)
76-248, 1976-1 C.B. 353	§§13.4(a), 15.5(e)	78-82, 1978-1 C.B. 70	§5.1(a)
76-296, 1976-2 C.B. 141	§5.3(a)	78-85, 1978-1 C.B. 150	§4.2
76-335, 1965-2 C.B. 141	§§10.4, 10.4(a)	78-90, 1978-1 C.B. 380	§16.3
76-336, 1976-2 C.B. 143	§5.1(a)	78-98, 1978-1 C.B. 167	§21.7(c)
76-354, 1976-2 C.B. 179	§21.12(b)	78-102, 1978-1 C.B. 379	§15.4(f)
76-384, 1976-2 C.B. 57	§5.1(a)	78-111	§23.4(a)
76-399, 1976-2 C.B. 147	§7.2(a)	78-112	§23.4(a)
76-401, 1976-2 C.B. 175	§8.2	78-113	§23.4(a)
76-402, 1976-2 C.B. 177	§21.7(c)	78-114, 1978-1 C.B. 41	§23.4(a)
76-410, 1976-2 C.B. 155	§8.4(b)	78-144, 1978-1 C.B. 168	§§15.1(c), 21.9(a)
76-416, 1976-2 C.B. 57	§11.2(f)	78-148, 1978-1C.B. 380	§15.4(g)
76-419, 1976-2 C.B. 146	§§4.2, 4.2(c)	78-225, 1978-1 C.B. 159	§§8.3(b), 8.8
76-420, 1976-2 C.B. 153	§7.1(c)	78-248, 1978-1 C.B. 154	§§23.2(a), 23.3(e)
76-424, 1976-2 C.B. 367	§13.2(a)	78-288, 1978-2 C.B. 179	§7.1(c)
76-440, 1976-2 C.B. 58	§11.2(h)	78-301, 1978-2 C.B. 103	§25.2(a)
76-441, 1967-2 C.B. 147	§20.5	78-305, 1978-2 C.B. 172	§§5.1, 5.1(e)
76-443, 1976-2 C.B. 149	§§5.1(g), 22.4(a)	78-315, 1978-2 C.B. 271	§15.5(b)
76-455, 1976-2 C.B. 150	§§8.4(a), 8.11	78-385, 1978-2 C.B. 174	§3.1(c)
76-456, 1976-2 C.B. 151	§23.2(b)	78-387, 1978-2 C.B. 270	§12.4(e)
76-459, 1976-2 C.B. 369	§14.7(b)	78-395, 1978-2 C.B. 270	§14.3(a)
76-460, 1976-2 C.B. 371	§17.3(a)	78-426, 1978-2 C.B. 175	§5.4
76-461, 1976-2 C.B. 371	§17.3(a)	78-428, 1978-2 C.B. 177	§§2.2(j), 4.1
77-1, 1977-1 C.B. 354	§15.4(g)	79-13, 1979-1 C.B. 208	§23.3(a)
77-4, 1977-1 C.B. 14	§5.1(j)	79-18, 1979-1 C.B. 152	§4.6(i)
77-7, 1977-1 C.B. 354	§15.4	79-71, 1968-1 C.B. 249	§5.1(e)
77-44, 1977-1 C.B. 118	§17.3(b)	79-128, 1979-1 C.B. 197	§6.3(b)
77-46, 1977-1 C.B. 147	§7.1(c)	79-145, 1979-1 C.B. 360	§9.1(b)
77-47, 1977-1 C.B. 156	§21.12(a)	79-167, 1979-1 C.B. 335	§5.1(a)
77-47, 1977-1 C.B. 157	§21.12(a)	79-319, 1979-2 C.B. 388	§15.4
77-111, 1977-1 C.B. 144	§§4.2, 4.2(c)	79-359, 1979-2 C.B. 226	§§3.1(c), 21.7(a),
77-112, 1977-1 C.B. 149	§8.2		24.1(a)
77-114, 1977-1 C.B. 153	§18.1(b)	79-360, 1979-2 C.B. 236	§4.6(g)

Revenue Rulings	Sections
79-369, 1979-2 C.B. 226	§21.7(a)
79-375, 1979-2 C.B. 389	§15.4(d)
80-63, 1980-1 C.B. 116	§6.4
80-69, 1980-1 C.B. 55	§24.1(b)
80-97, 1980-1 C.B. 257	§17.7
80-110, 1980-16 IRB 10	§25.2(b)
80-114	§21.7(a)
80-118, 1980-1 C.B. 254	§13.1(b)
80-132, 1980-1 C.B. 255	§14.3(a)
80-133, 1980-1 C.B. 258	§16.2(b)
80-205, 1980-1 C.B. 184	§6.2
80-206, 1980-2 C.B. 185	§6.2
80-215, 1980-2 C.B. 174	§§5.1(e), 5.5
80-278, 1980-2 C.B. 175	§4.2
80-279, 1980-2 C.B. 176	§4.2
80-282, 1980-2 C.B. 154	§23.2(a)
80-286, 1980-2 C.B. 179	§4.5, 5.1(e)
80-287, 1980-2 C.B. 185	§§8.4(a), 8.11
80-295	§21.7(c)
80-296	§21.7(c)
80-301, 1980-2 C.B. 180	§2.2(a)
80-302, 1980-2 C.B. 182	§2.2(a)
80-310, 1980-2 C.B. 319	§14.5(e)
81-29, 1981-1 C.B. 328	§2.2(j)
81-29, 1981-1 C.B. 329	§§4.5, 21.7(a), 21.8(b)
81-40, 1981-1 C.B. 508	§§14.2(b), 14.10(a)
81-40, 1981-1 C.B. 509	§14.10(a)
81-46. 1981-1 C.B. 514	§17.3(f)
81-60, 1981-1 C.B. 335	§8.7
81-61, 1981-1 C.B. 355	§22-4(c)
81-69, 1981-1 C.B. 351	§9.5(c)
81-94, 1981-1 C.B. 330	§3.2
81-95, 1981-1 C.B. 332	§§6.1, 23.1(a)
81-101, 1981-1 C.B. 352	§21.15(c)
81-108, 1980-1 C.B. 327	§10.4(a)
81-125, 1981-1 C.B. 515	§17.4(a)
81-127, 1981-1 C.B. 357	§8.4(a)
81-138, 1981-1 C.B. 358	§§8.8, 21.12(a)
81-175, 1981-1 C.B. 337	§8.4(b)
81-178, 1981-2 C.B. 135	§§21.8(c), 21.10(d)
81-178, 1981-2 C.B. 137	§21.10(d)
81-217, 1981-2 C.B. 217	§17.3(g)
81-276, 1981-2 C.B. 128	§4.6(h)
81-284, 1981-2 C.B. 130	§4.2(c)
81-295, 1981-2 C.B. 15	§21.9(f)
81-811, 1981-1 C.B. 509	§16.1(b)

Revenue Rulings	Sections
82-136, 1982-2 C.B. 300	§14.5(e)
82-137, 1982-2 C.B. 303	§15.1(d)
82-138, 1982-2 C.B. 106	§8.6
82-223, 1982-2 C.B. 301	§§14.5(a), 17.7
83-74, 1983-1 C.B. 112	§§6.4(a), 6.4(c)
83-104, 1983-2 C.B. 46	§24.1(a)
83-120, 1983-2 C.B. 170	§ 20.7
83-153, 1983-2 C.B. 48	§11.5(c)
83-157, 1983-2 C.B. 94	§4.6(a)
83-164, 1983-2 C.B. 95	§8.3(a)
83-170, 1983-2 C.B. 97	§9.1(b)
84-41, 1984-1 C.B. 130	§21.8(i)
84-169, 1984-2 C.B. 216	§13.6
85-1, 1985-1 C.B. 177	§4.3
85-2, 1985-1 C.B. 178	§4.3
85-162, 1985-2 C.B. 275	§14.5(e)
86-23, 1986-1 C.B. 564	§3.2(c)
86-63, 1986-1 C.B. 88	§24.1(a)
86-95, 1986-2 C.B. 73	§23.2(a)
86-98, 1986-2 C.B. 74	§6.2
87-2, 1987-1 C.B. 18	§10.3(e)
87-41, 1987-1 C.B. 296	§25.1
87-119, 1987-2 C.B. 151	§23.3(a)
88-56, 1988-2 C.B. 126	§6.4(a)
93-84, 1993-39 IRB 4	§13.2(a)
94-16, 1994-1 C.B. 19	§21.9(f)
95-8, 1995-4 IRB 29	§21.12(a)
95-8, 1995-14 IRB 1	§21.10(b)
97-21, 1997-18 IRB 115	§§4.6(b), 4.6(c)
98-15	§22.2(b)
98-15, 1998-12 IRB	§4.6(b)
98-19, 1998-1 C.B. 840	§24.1(a)
99-44, 1999-2 C.B. 549	§24.1(a)
2002-28, 2002-1 C.B. 941	§12.4
2002-43, 2002-28 IRB 85	§14.3(a)
2002-44, 2002-28 IRB 84	§13.2(a)
2003-12, 2003-1 C.B. 283	§§24.1(a), 25.1(e)
2003-13, 2003-1 C.B. 305	§12.4(c)
2003-32, 2003-14 C.B. 689	§17.3(e)
2003-99, 2003-34 IRB 388	§5.1(e)
2004-6, 2004-4 IRB 328	§23.3(e)
2004-112, 2004-51 IRB 985	§21.9(e)
2005-46, 2005-30 IRB 120	§24.1(a)
2006-27, 2006-21 IRB 915	§4.2(b)
2007-41, 200-25 IRB 1421	§23.3(e)
2009-9, 2009-14 IRB 735	§§13.3(a), 13.4(b)

Table of IRS Procedures

Revenue Procedures	Sections	Revenue Procedures	Sections
71-17, 1971-1 CB 390	§9.4(b)	96-40, 1996-32 IRB 8	§18.2(f)
71-17, 1971-1 C.B. 683	§9.3(c)	97-12, 1997-1 C.B. 631	§7.1(e)
72-5, 1972-1 C.B. 709	§3.4	97-12, 1997-4 IRB 1	§8.6
75-50, 1975-2 C.B. 587	§5.1(b)	98-16, 1998-5 IRB	§24.1(e)
76-47, 1976-2 C.B. 670	§17.3(e)	98-19, 1998-1 C.B. 547	§7.4
77-32, 1977-2 C.B. 541	§17.3(e)	98-25, 1989-1 C.B. 79	§17.4
80-27, 1980-1 C.B. 677	§18.1(d)	2001-59, 2001-52 IRB 627	§6.5(a)
80-39, 1980-2 C.B. 772	§17.3(e)	2002-64, 2002-2 CB 17	§10.2
81-6, 1981-1 C.B. 620	§17.4(d)	2003-12, 2003-1 CB 316	§2.1(b)
81-7, 1981-1 C.B. 621	§11.2(h)	2003-34, 2003-18 IRB 856	§18.3(b)
81-65	§17.3(e)	2003-45	§18.3(b)
81-65, 1981-2 C.B. 690	§17.3(e)	2003-79	§18.3(b)
82-2, 1982-1 C.B. 367	§§2.1(b), 2.1(g)	2003-85, 2003-49 IRB 1184	§7.2(c)
82-39, 1982-17 IRB 18	§18.1(f)	2007-58, 2007 ???	§7.4
83-32	§12.3	2007-66, 2007-7CB 970	§24.2(c)
85-51, 1985-2 C.B. 717	§17.3(e)	2008-55, 2008-39 IRB 768	§17.4(a)
85-58, 1985-2 C.B. 740	§18.3(b)	_____, 2009-1 IRB 229	§18.1
86-43, 1986-2 C.B. 729	§§5.1, 5.1(k)	2009-21, 2009-16 IRB 860	§§7.2(c), 7.4
89-23, 1989-1 C.B. 844	§17.4(d)	2010-9, 2010.2 IRB 256	§18.0
90-12	§§21.9(g), 24.3(a)	2010-40	§21.9(g)
90-27, 1990-1 C.B. 514	§18.1(b)	2010-40, 2010-46 IRB 663	§§6.5(f), 21.8(e),
91-20, 1991-10 IRB 26	§3.3		24.2(b), 24.3(a)
92-59, 1992-29 IRB 11	§4.2(d)	2011-1	§18.3(a)
92-94, 1992-2 C.B. 507	§17.3(d)	2011-8	§12.4(d)
92-94, 1992-46 IRB 34	§§17.5(b), 17.5(c)	2011-8, 2011-1 IRB 237	§§12.4(g), 17.3(f),
94-78, 1994-52 IRB 38	§17.3(e)		18.3(a)
95-21, 1995-15 IRB 1	§§7.1(e), 8.6	2011-9, 2011-2 IRB 283	§18.1(f)
95-48, 1995-2 C.B. 418	§10.3(g)	2011-10, 2011-2 IRB 294	§11.5(f)
95-48, 1995-47 IRB 13	§§10.2, 10.3(c),	2011-15, 2011-3 IRB 322	§13.6
	18.2(d),	2011-33, 2011-25 IRB ___	§18.1(f)
	20.10(a)	2011-36, 2011-25 IRB 915	§17.3(f)
96-10, 1996-1 C.B. 577	§3.2(c)	2017-58	§7.4
96-11, 1996-1C.B. 577	§18.2(d)	2019-22	§_____
96-32, 1996-20 IRB 1	§4.2(a)		

Index